# Right Texts, Wrong Meanings

# Right Texts, Wrong Meanings

Busting Myths from Popular New Testament Texts

SAM TSANG

WIPF & STOCK · Eugene, Oregon

RIGHT TEXTS, WRONG MEANINGS
Busting Myths from Popular New Testament Texts

Copyright © 2013 Sam Tsang. All rights reserved. Except for brief quotations in critical publications or reviews, no part of this book may be reproduced in any manner without prior written permission from the publisher. Write: Permissions, Wipf and Stock Publishers, 199 W. 8th Ave., Suite 3, Eugene, OR 97401.

Wipf & Stock
An Imprint of Wipf and Stock Publishers
199 W. 8th Ave., Suite 3
Eugene, OR 97401
www.wipfandstock.com

ISBN 13: 978-1-62032-733-3
Manufactured in the U.S.A.

All Scripture quotations, unless otherwise noted, are taken from THE HOLY BIBLE, NEW INTERNATIONAL VERSION®, NIV® Copyright © 1973, 1978, 1984, 2011 by Biblica, Inc.™ Used by permission. All rights reserved worldwide.

*To my colleagues at Hong Kong Baptist Theological Seminary*

# Contents

*Acknowledgments ix*
*Introduction xi*

## Part One: Popularly Misused Texts in Narrative

1. Matthew 7:1–12: To Judge or Not? 3
2. Matthew 11:28–30: Finding "Rest" in Jesus? 10
3. Matthew 18: Church Discipline? Prayer Meetings? 17
4. Mark 6:14–29: A Gruesome Murder Only? 23
5. Mark 11:22–25: Prayers that Move Mountains? 28
6. Luke 2:1–20: The "Humble" Baby Jesus? 33
7. Luke 6:17–26: Poverty as the Ultimate Good? 38
8. Luke 10:38–42: Submissive Mary Against Fussy Martha? 44
9. Luke 11:1–13: The Lord's Prayer Only? 52
10. Luke 15: Which Lost Son? 57
11. Luke 16:1–15: Dishonesty and Divorce? 62
12. Luke 21:1–4: A Lesson on Sacrificial Giving? 72
13. John 10:1–21: A Lesson about Shepherding? 77

## Part Two: Popularly Misused Texts in Letters

14. Romans 8:28: All Things Work Out? 89
15. Romans 13: Absolute Obedience to an Unjust Government? 96

Contents

16　1 Corinthians 6:12–20: My Body, God's Temple?　102

17　1 Corinthians 11:1: Imitate Paul, Imitate Christ?　109

18　2 Corinthians 6:14: Unequally Yoked, Unequally Married?　115

19　Ephesians 2:14: Which Wall?　121

20　Ephesians 2:20: Prophets Today?　127

21　Ephesians 6:10–18: Putting on the Full Armor of God?　132

22　Philippians 2:5: Same Attitude as Christ's?　137

23　1 Timothy 4:8: An Excuse *Not* to Keep Fit?　141

24　2 Timothy 3:16: "All" Scripture Is "God-Breathed?"　145

25　James 3:1–2: Watching Your Tongue?　149

**PART THREE: POPULARLY MISUSED TEXTS IN APOCALYPTIC LITERATURE**

26　Revelation 3:16, 20: Lukewarm? An Invitation to Unbelievers?　155

27　Revelation 7:1–17; 14:1–5: Israel and the Rapture Church?　162

28　Revelation 22:18–19: Subtracting from the Canon?　169

Conclusion　173

# Acknowledgments

MANY HAVE CONTRIBUTED TO my intellectual and spiritual development, evident in the great cloud of witnesses that has written recommendations for the back cover of this book. They have become examples for me to emulate. Recent years at Hong Kong Baptist Theological Seminary have also afforded me the chance to work among some fine colleagues. My stint in Hong Kong gave me valuable exposure to academic needs beyond North America. I especially want to thank my copy editor Timothy McNinch for his editing. I also want to thank Dr. Daniel Cheung of the University of Dayton Philosophy department, who gave my manuscript a quick "once over" to see if there were any logical fallacies. Wipf and Stock deserves a mention simply because they've taken a chance on my first book with them. While I have published some of this material in a different form for my Chinese readers under Logos Ministries in Hong Kong,[1] I'm glad to have my shot to influence the English readership now. For all of the above, I give thanks. I also thank God for the gift of family, my wife Helen and my two sons, Calvin and Ian. They've tolerated my many shortcomings and made me a better man.

---

1. Tsang, Sam. *Commonly Misinterpreted Texts*. Hong Kong: Logos, 2011.

# Introduction

I START MY INTRODUCTION with a set of test questions:
- Does Matthew 7:1 mean not to judge?
- Is the lost son in Luke 15 the younger son?
- Is Romans 13 about the absolute obedience to the government?
- Is the term "lukewarm" a description of spiritual temperature in Revelation 3:16?
- Is the widow's mite in Luke 21:1–4 about giving?

If you answered "yes" to any of these, you need this book.

Fortunately or unfortunately, I was nourished on evangelical preaching and Sunday school from birth. As a result, I've heard some really fantastic sermons and lessons—but also some not-so-good ones. The more I think about the number of bad examples, the more passages I find filling up the pages of this book. There is simply a whole lot wrong with today's average Bible study and pulpit. Some do not even flip a Bible open at all, but instead tell entertaining anecdotes and stories to fill up that dreadful (sometimes "dreaded") half hour. I hope this work rectifies some misunderstood verses among both preachers and the laity.

This is not a scholarly work. While some academic books deal with the technical aspects, this book will point the way for lay Bible readers. I hope this book reaches those who find technical books too difficult, but still want to read the Bible with care. My wish is to write a book that appeals to non-academic readers so that they can learn some easy ways to check and balance varying interpretations.

My title for each passage, stated in the form of a question, is deliberately controversial. Almost all the answers to the questions are a resounding "no" or a hesitant "not really." This book is meant to provoke critical thinking about virtually all usages of scripture quotation. I believe lay people without a formal theological education are capable of judging whether or

## Introduction

not a speaker or book is biblical in its scriptural usage. Critical thinking is not for the expert only!

My method is simple—in fact, too simple. As simple as this book is, somebody has to write it. In each case, I merely try to first nail down the proper literary, contextual beginning and ending of the story or passage. Then I put the passage and its meaning within its book context. I also set the text within the historical background of the book, when necessary. The very same process applies to passages from letters, also. The meaning, of course, is based on what the original audience knew. So I sometimes address the question of the audience's situation.

Since this book aims directly at a lay audience, I have only included very basic and accessible discussions on Greek. I do not presuppose that my readers know Greek. Even without knowing Greek, we can go a long away in understanding the Bible, if our methods and presuppositions are right. We can even do reasonable and well-reasoned Bible studies and daily readings, if we grasp the methods in this book. When we read these familiar verses in context, their meanings become much more profound than popularly understood. That's my belief.

The purpose of this book is not polemical. The selection of passages however is based on what I have heard in sermons throughout my years of attending church. I hope to make discovering biblical truth we take for granted fun again. These days, the church's focus seems to be on anything other than biblical literacy. As a result, even churches that claim to be biblical are often very unbiblical. Hopefully, in journeying through this book, my readers will rediscover the joy of reading the text based on its context, taking any traditional explanation with a grain of salt.

There are many misunderstood verses besides the examples I use in this book. Perhaps, some readers may prefer other examples, but I have written to show the process by which I arrive at my interpretations. I show how taking context seriously can take us a long way to the meaning of any given New Testament text. The method is often the key to clear understanding. Some essays are longer than others simply because some passages involve much wider contexts than others. Through these examples, I hope to illustrate step-by-step deterrence from committing common interpretive mistakes. I also include an application section after each analysis to show not only the relevance of each text, but also how a sound method can give spiritual direction to a believer's life.

*Introduction*

The book is divided into three large parts. The first is narrative, the second is letters, and the third is apocalyptic. Within narratives, I include Jesus' sermons. It is a mistake to see these sermons as a separate genre when they are buried within narratives. By not considering the narrative context, as some interpreters fail to do, Jesus' sermons lose their meanings. The second section, the letters, shows how they also demand a careful reading of their context. The third section, the apocalyptic literature, namely Revelation, demands a bit more than just a mere reading. I shall explain more fully when we get there.

Each chapter in this book is composed of six parts in order to walk my readers through the process from reading to application. First, I start with the popular meaning in our churches. I realize that there are many possible meanings, but I put down the most popular meanings. Second, I explore where each passage in question begins and ends so that we have a scope to work with. My readers will discover one truth: the traditional chapter and verse divisions are not original to the biblical authors. This simple observation will illuminate many of our interpretations. Third, I introduce my interpretation of the passage by a careful reading of the text. Fourth, I look at how the whole passage applies to our faith community and our individual ethics. Fifth, I discuss where interpretative mistakes are made and how to avoid them. Sixth and finally, I include a set of questions for spiritual formation of the believer, or for small group discussions in faith communities. All biblical references are taken from the New International Version.

# 1

## Matthew 7:1–12—
## To Judge or Not?

"Do not judge, or you too will be judged. For in the same way you judge others, you will be judged, and with the measure you use, it will be measured to you.

"Why do you look at the speck of sawdust in your brother's eye and pay no attention to the plank in your own eye? How can you say to your brother, 'Let me take the speck out of your eye,' when all the time there is a plank in your own eye? You hypocrite, first take the plank out of your own eye, and then you will see clearly to remove the speck from your brother's eye.

"Do not give dogs what is sacred; do not throw your pearls to pigs. If you do, they may trample them under their feet, and turn and tear you to pieces.

"Ask and it will be given to you; seek and you will find; knock and the door will be opened to you. For everyone who asks receives; the one who seeks finds; and to the one who knocks, the door will be opened.

"Which of you, if your son asks for bread, will give him a stone? Or if he asks for a fish, will give him a snake? If you, then, though you are evil, know how to give good gifts to your children, how much more will your Father in heaven give good gifts to those who ask him! So in everything, do to others what you would have them do to you, for this sums up the Law and the Prophets."

# Right Texts, Wrong Meanings

## THE POPULAR MEANING

I SAW A FACEBOOK update that said, "Thou shall not judge others by their Facebook updates." Without a doubt, Matthew 7:1 is popular.

There are three common meanings given for 7:1–12. Let me list them as simply as possible. We shall see later that these three popular meanings mislead rather than enlighten.

First, 7:1 is often quoted like some kind of proverb, even for Facebook updates. Basically the popular interpretation goes something like this: If you judge others, you will also be judged by God. So, absolutely do not judge under any circumstances.

Second, 7:6 is often applied in terms of evangelism strategy. The interpretation goes something like this: If we give a message to a potential convert, and they refuse to believe, then we treat them like dogs and pigs.

Third, 7:7–12 is a passage that is frequently misunderstood because it seems to contain teaching on prayer. The common interpretation goes something like this: Jesus wants us to pray so much that we pray without ceasing, like asking, seeking, and knocking. Eventually, we can change God's mind through our persistence. Where Does the Passage Begin?

Before we find the true meaning of this passage, we must first find out where it begins. It is easy to assume the passage begins at 7:1. However, I like to see it as part of a bigger picture of worldview discussion. (My readers will have to indulge me a bit for this detailed discussion. The paradigm I create from this discussion will determine how we view the verses in question.) If we see no logical coherence, but just view these as separate topics or just see them as a collection of Jesus' teachings compiled by Matthew for no particular reason, we probably have not tried hard enough. Logical coherence is the key.

It is important to recognize the connecting points in any sermon, the places where sections change. In this passage, the best place to see a blatant change is 6:25, where Jesus said, "therefore," drawing to a close the discussion on doing acts of righteousness in front of others (found in 6:1–18) and storing up the right treasures (6:19–24). If the section 6:19–24 draws the discussion to a close, then it not only points directly towards the discussion about acts of righteousness, but is an indispensible part of it.

The discussion that follows the "therefore" in 6:25 has a series of prohibitions that start with "do not . . ." Matthew 7:1 continues this series of prohibitions. It is as if Jesus was saying that the reason people did acts of righteousness in front of others was because they sought worldly value rather than kingdom value. Such false acts of self-righteousness may lead to a judgmental attitude towards others. We must however look at how the entire chapter 6 coheres together, in order to understand how chapter 7 follows.

The worldly value the people sought went directly against the three acts of righteousness. They sought worldly value because they did not believe God would reward them for their secret, but generous, giving (cf. 6:4), for their secret, but faith-based, prayer (cf. 6:6, 8), and for their secret, but truthful, fasting (cf. 6:18). This will be important in understanding the subsequent discussion of 7:1–12. The repeated theme of God being a rewarding God goes completely against the worldview of those who sought worldly reward, whether in material gain or human approval. The acts of righteousness from 6:1–24 indicate the kind of belief people had in God. The logic looks something like this outline:

| 6:1 | acts of righteousness |
| --- | --- |
| 6:2–4 | correct judgment about God and others in giving results in two kinds of reward |
| 6:5–15 | correct judgment about God and others in prayer results in two kinds of reward |
| 6:16–18 | correct judgment about God and others in fasting results in two kinds of reward |

Part of 7:1–12 complements 6:1–24 because of the logical progression of the former into the latter:

| 6:1–24 | acts of righteousness |
| --- | --- |
| 7:1–12 | self-righteousness |

From the above diagram, the logic shows that acts of righteousness, if not done with the correct attitude, can lead to self-righteousness.

In other words, 6:1–24 has to do with how others and God judge the kingdom citizen, while 7:1–12 is about how the citizen judges others. Thus, the self-righteousness of 7:1 is rooted in the self-glorification of 6:1–18. Such self-glorification is rooted in a lack of understanding of the God of this kingdom, stated in 6:19–34. We cannot understand what goes on after 7:1 without looking back at 6:1–18 and the transitional connection of 6:19–34.

## THE MEANING OF THE PASSAGE

Having looked briefly at the sectional division, I think we're ready to dive in and find the meaning for 7:1–12. Right at 7:1, Jesus addressed the audience in second person plural "you," which shows his intention to set them apart from others. From whom would they be set apart? There is a hint that Jesus was talking to a person with the attitude of the self-righteous Pharisee because Jesus used his favorite polemical description, "hypocrites," in 7:5 (cf. 6:2, 5, 16). Additionally, "hypocrites" was a favorite description by Jesus of the Pharisees in Matthew (e.g., 15:7; 22:18; 23:13, 15, 23, 25, 27; etc.). The word "hypocrites" takes on a very negative connotation, but it actually means something like "play actors." It only (rightly) takes on a negative connotation because the person acting out righteousness is not, in reality, very righteous at all.

Now that we have seen the wider context of the hypocrites, let's look at the two analogies Jesus used in order to illustrate 7:1–2. First, Jesus used the plank and sawdust analogy, but he also individualized the application by switching from the plural "you" in 7:1 to singular "you" in 7:3 to show personal responsibility playing a part in kingdom value. The singular "you" continues all the way to Matthew 7:3–5. As an example, the verses in Matthew 7:1–3 look something like this:

7:1 Do not judge, or you (plural) too will be judged.

7:2 For in the same way you (plural) judge others, you (plural) will be judged, and with the measure you (plural) use, it will be measured to you (plural).

7:3 Why do you (singular) look at the speck of sawdust in your (singular) brother's eye and pay no attention to the plank in your (singular) own eye?

By switching from general corporate command to individual responsibility, Jesus was saying that every kingdom citizen can become a hypocrite. The key to taking responsibility has to do with vision. In Matthew 7:4, when Jesus discussed the singular "eye," he was not talking about a person having only one eye, but he was talking about impaired vision because of the plank. In today's example, it is like getting a two-by-four in the eye socket. With the plank in one eye, only one eye could see. Furthermore, if a plank was through an eye socket, the impaired vision could be potentially deadly. A plank through the eye socket is fatal!

By comparing the plank with the sawdust, Jesus not only demonstrated existence of two similar problems, but also different degrees of the problem. To judge others for the same fault we commit is the very definition of hypocrisy. To judge others for the same fault, while having a similar flaw to a greater degree, is completely foolhardy. The very fact a plank is in one's eye shows how readily obvious and painful our own fault is. Jesus was saying that if his listeners still did not notice such an obviously painful reality in their own eyes, then they were even in worse shape than originally thought. The willingness to execute critical self-judgment is highly important. Moreover, Jesus did not say that the judgment was merely self-judgment, but may also come in the form of correction by others. He said that when people did not pay attention to the plank, it opened the possibility for others to notice the plank. In other words, others could comment and say, "Hey, you have a plank there." The impaired vision caused misjudgment about the seriousness of one's own problem. The plank could cause one to lose his life altogether. Contrary to common misconception, Jesus was not saying that we should never judge. Rather, he was saying that no judgment should be executed without prior self-judgment. Judgment can be proper only when the moral standing and vision are grounded in true righteousness.

In suggesting that we correctly remove the sawdust from the brother's eye, Jesus implied that the brother is willing for the sawdust to be removed. The person is open for correction and self-betterment. However, what if a person is unwilling to change, even if correct judgment is cast upon him? The answer leads us to Jesus' second analogy in 7:6. Jesus' answer was to not cast or give what is precious to dogs and pigs, both of which were unclean in first-century Jewish culture. Many commentators do not know how to deal with 7:6. The answers must lie in the context, along with the switch from second person singular of previous verses to plural in 7:6. Therefore, the community and not merely the individual should decide whether a person is a dog or a pig. "What is sacred" denotes whatever is set apart by the sacred community of Jesus, especially regarding truth and judgment. This ceremonial language describes not so much sacrificial meat, but that which is given in form of truth, especially correcting a "brother" (7:3–5). Within the context, this is not talking about evangelism strategy, as it has been so commonly presupposed, but about dealing with an erring brother.

It is best to summarize what we have found so far. The first analogy of the plank and sawdust deals with the person making judgment. The second analogy of dogs and pigs deals with the person receiving the judgment.

Thus, judgment involves first the person doing the judging but also involves a further reflection of the person who "should" receive the judgment. If neither scenario is ideal, then we must refrain from judgment.

The next part, starting from 7:7, seems to be about prayer. But we shall see that it is not really about prayer. Jesus was using it to continue his teaching about judging. Two facts help lead me to this conclusion: the redundant teaching about prayer here, in comparison to 6:5–15, and the odd placement of the "Golden Rule" (7:12) in terms of the teaching of 7:7–11.

Now that Jesus had given the right context of judging, he turned his attention to the human's relationship with God through prayer. Having already dealt with prayer in 6:5–15, why should he talk about prayer again? He had a very good reason. The first hint to help us understand why Jesus taught about prayer is the use of the plural "you" here. The application is certainly not to individuals but to the whole community as Jesus continued to use the plural "you." Prayer, then, should be for communal edification and not for individual amusement. Together, perhaps the community can make a sound judgment (7:1–6) in a prayerful manner. Prayer and judgment, then, ought to be related somehow.

Jesus first stated the general principle of answered prayer in 7:7–8. Jesus moved from ask, to seek, to knock. The Greek here can express "keep on asking, keep on seeking, keep on knocking." To ask implies a face-to-face conversation. To seek implies that something is hidden. To knock means there is something in the way of getting what one wants. Asking involves words. Seeking involves the feet and the whole person to look for something. Knocking involves judging that something or someone is behind closed doors. The urgency from asking to knocking seems to intensify. We shall see how all this is related to judging later.

In his usual fashion of illustrating commands with analogies, Jesus turned to human behavior in 7:9–10. This behavior should be intimately linked with the discussion on dogs and pigs in regard to judgment. He dealt with the way human sons ask for things from their fathers. Jesus used the plural "you" in "which of you" to indicate this not only as an individual case, but as normal communal human behavior (he was obviously excluding abnormal and abusive cases). In using this analogy, Jesus actually hid a principle that will be clearly stated in subsequent passages. Jesus used bread and fish and compared them with stone and snake. The parallelism here is quite informative.

When interpreting such a passage, it helps to have an active imagination to understand what Jesus was talking about. We can do so by imagining the picture Jesus was painting. If the son asks for bread, he should get bread. If he gets stone, that would be abnormal. The same can be said of the fish and snake. The analogy stirs the imagination because bread resembles a stone while a fish resembles a snake. Thus, sometimes what seems to be bread is a stone and what seems to be a fish is a snake. In the same way that sacred things are not good or fit for dogs, neither are pearls good for swine. Such is the nature of answered prayer. Jesus was saying to his Jewish audience that only God could always tell which was which. For God, the gifts are always bread and fish, and not stone and snake. The gifts are never bad for us. The Father always gives good gifts! Yet, the recipient does not always know how to distinguish between things that seem similar, but are diametrically different.

It is important to pay attention to the prayer teaching because it is part of the judging topic without any hint of a break. In light of the context of judgment in 7:1–6, Jesus' teaching on prayer here is unique. The message is clear: if God is so good to us, we can surely be generous with our brothers who have stumbled. Grace is the highest standard God has set. So, instead of judging quickly without self-examination first, and even allowing others to examine us, we should judge cautiously and never judge without the same kind of grace God extends to his children. The whole discussion about judgment in 7:1–6 is missing one element: grace. The section 7:7–12 adds the missing element to complete the discussion.

Jesus finally concluded with the so-called "Golden Rule" in 7:12. First, the Rule acts as a fitting conclusion to what has been started in 7:1, thus implying that all of 7:1–12 should be read together somehow. It is virtually a general restatement of 7:1. It also ties in well with 7:7–11. Unfortunately, many readers have chosen to apply the teaching on prayer as some kind of separate saying and some kind of general maxim for daily living. The section of 7:7–11 tells us that God is a good giver. In the light of good gifts from God, 7:12 encourages us to be careful about how to deal with others, not in a hypocritical and judgmental manner but in a gracious manner. If God gives us such great things, we should also treat others well. If we mistreat others, we are acting as unbecoming recipients of God's grace. The interpersonal relationships between kingdom citizens have their basis on the showering of goodness towards one another, because God has freely given to us first. Our relationships with others show us our own understanding of God's grace. It is now time to look at how Jesus' sermon fits in the overall narrative of Matthew.

How in fact should this be read in the light of the whole of Matthew 5–7? We may notice the overwhelming usage of the plural "you," which denotes some kind of community rather than individuals. Jesus was viewing an individual citizen of the kingdom in light of a community. Relational health reflects the citizen's kingdom status. As the sermon heading a series of five sermons in Matthew, Jesus was using his words here to build a new community of the kingdom, before he moved on to other matters of the kingdom. Thus, this gracious relational treatment of one another leads to greater things in the kingdom.

How does the passage work in terms of the narrative context of Matthew? Within Matthew, God's judgment occurs in the eschaton (19:28; 26:31–33, 46). Although judgment belongs almost exclusively to the future in Matthew, the church's community needs to make correct judgment calls about their own situations, according to the standard set forth by the heavenly Father. The church and her members should not be involved in petty self-righteous judgment. The church can represent the future hope clearly even in this life by making the right judgment call, not against others, but first and foremost against her members to make sure that all members are making the right judgment about themselves before calling others into judgment. The higher standard of representing God also requires a large dose of grace, the way God grants grace to imperfect children who want things that are good for them.

## APPLICATIONS

In dealing with the first common misunderstanding, Jesus was not forbidding judgment. After correct self-examination and examination by others, the kingdom citizen would know which is a dog and which is a pig even within the faith community. Jesus gave two conditions for judging. First, he made sure the kingdom citizen does not have blind spots. Second, he made sure the recipient of the judgment was ready to hear correction.

In dealing with the second common misunderstanding, Jesus was not talking about evangelism, but about correcting a brother. In other words, this passage is more about what we do within the community, but not necessarily what the community does with outsiders.

In dealing with the third common misunderstanding, Jesus was not teaching about prayer, but about the goodness of God, using the topic of prayer as an illustration. This topic encourages the children of God to act with God's mercy towards their brothers and sisters by giving them good things in dealing with their faults. God's goodness can often be experienced by our relationships. Thus, God's grace should mark all relationships.

*Matthew 7:1–12—To Judge or Not?*

The teaching, then, is about the identity of the community. The Christian community needs to mirror the relationship between God and his children. That same relationship is already evident in chapter six, where God is the reward giver of righteous acts. Quite often, we use the metaphor "Father" to describe God. Without understanding this father as a reward giver, it is hard to make the right judgment about self and others. In our egalitarian society with many dysfunctional family relationships, maybe "father" is not the best metaphor for grace. No matter what metaphor we use to describe this great relationship between God and his children, people cannot see God's generous grace until our relationships demonstrate it. The community that identifies with God will exhibit God's goodness.

## MISTAKES TO AVOID

The above three misunderstandings bring out the importance of cutting the paragraphs correctly. The material prior to this teaching within the sermon should guide interpretation of the passage. The sermon ought to be viewed as one piece. The separate pieces are each only one part of the puzzle. God's character in chapter 6 still guides how we behave in chapter 7. Moreover, we need to take seriously the fact that there is little information about Matthew's audience. The reader may notice that I did not guess at the kind of historical audience to which Matthew was writing. I believe guessing at the audience situation is a worthwhile historical reconstructive endeavor, though it may or may not be helpful in getting the most basic message within the text. Too much is unknown for the purpose of our exercise here. In Gospel sermons, sometimes the text is all we have.

## DISCUSSION QUESTIONS

- What are the problems facing the three common meanings for the text?
- What does prayer have to do with judging?
- How does the "Golden Rule" apply to judging?
- How does knowledge of God's character in both chapters 6 and 7 guide us in dealing with others?
- In what practical ways can our faith community find balance between not judging at all and judging correctly?

# 2

# Matthew 11:28–30— Finding "Rest" in Jesus?

"Come to me, all you who are weary and burdened, and I will give you rest. Take my yoke upon you and learn from me, for I am gentle and humble in heart, and you will find rest for your souls. For my yoke is easy and my burden is light."

## THE POPULAR MEANING

MOST AMERICANS FIND THEIR stress level moving up every year. While the economics of this country do not help, I attribute this stress level to a lack of faith in Jesus. Once people receive Jesus' great invitation to find rest in him from Matthew 11:28–30, they will surely feel better.

The above sermonic plot is the very typical interpretation of this text. Christianity is the big escape from all of life's problems. The trouble is, what if our faith does not allow us to escape life's problems? What then?

We shall see below that the popular interpretation is not the correct one and it generalizes unnecessarily, to the detriment of Christian spiritual formation.

## WHERE DOES THE PASSAGE BEGIN?

The passage naturally starts at 11:2. It is a response to John the Baptist's query about Jesus' messianic status. The ending of the passage, however, seems a lot more puzzling. The first hint that 12:1 is a continuation of Matthew 11 is the phrase "at that time," found both in 11:25 and 12:1. The narrator seems to draw attention to this parallel to show that the passage has not yet ended. The chronological note seems to link the passages together. "At that time" should cause us to ask, "At *what* time?" The answer naturally causes us to look back at the event described in chapter 11. If the event has not ended, the entire event should be interpreted together. As sensible readers of narrative, we do not stop reading until the narrative ends. Modern authors do not just tell half a story and cut it off with no ending. Why should we expect the biblical authors to do otherwise? Thus, we should base our decision about where the passage divides on the occasion of the event, and not the traditional division. Matthew was recording live events, not chapters and verses.[1]

When reading Matthew, there are times when the overall structure becomes even more important. Matthew is divided by five sermons (chapters 5–7, 10, 13, 18, 24–25) surrounded by narratives that are more or less related. Chapters 5–7 introduce Jesus' kingdom ministry. What follows is the demonstration of that ministry. Chapter 10 shows the sending of the disciples as the real Israel. The subsequent chapters show what the real Israel would be like. Chapter 13 shows the nature of the kingdom with parables that say, "The kingdom of heaven is like . . ." The demonstration of that kingdom happens in the events that follow until chapter 18. Chapter 18 talks about the members of the kingdom followed by demonstration of what these members looked like. Finally, chapters 24–25 show the culmination of the kingdom related to Jerusalem. The subsequent section shows Jesus' passion in relation to Jerusalem. The king would be rejected in Jerusalem but he would triumph. By his triumph, he would remain true to his judgment, as he promised in chapters 24–25. Matthew 11–12 belongs to the narrative portion before Matthew 13, which contains a sermon. Matthew 11–12 also belongs after the sermon of Matthew 10, which discusses the mission of the kingdom. Thus, the little sermon here (not one of the five big sermons) and its lessons have to connect to the surrounding narratives.

---

1. Let me reiterate that the earliest Bibles did not have chapter and verse divisions. Chapter divisions were added beginning in the thirteenth century, and verse divisions did not appear until after the Reformation.

## THE MEANING OF THE PASSAGE

The meaning of 11:28–30 must first be derived from the immediately embedded sermon of 11:4–30. I say "embedded" because it does not belong to the five big sermons, but it is a saying of Jesus embedded within a narrative. In other words, 11:4–30 is embedded within the narrative that starts at 11:2–3. Thus, the narrative context ought to dictate the meaning of Jesus' sermon. It is not merely a set of teachings but a response to the narrative situation. The narrative plot looks something like this.

| 11:1–3 | occasion of John's imprisonment and his question |
| 11:4–19 | Jesus' answer to John's question |
| 11:20–24 | Jesus' denouncement of the cities |
| 11:25–30 | Jesus' prayer and call |

In 11:2–3, the question from the imprisoned John was, "Are you the one who was to come, or should we expect someone else?"

Jesus' response was very direct in 11:4–6, in which he showed through various ministries he had done that he was indeed the one who was to come. Following the discussion about himself and John, Jesus then roundly condemned some of the major Galilean cities in 11:21–24. This condemnation ought to be considered a result of their indiscriminate rejection of Jesus' work.

After addressing the crowd, Jesus turned his attention to his Father in 11:25–26. Without indicating a break with a statement like "and Jesus addressed the crowd," Matthew resumed Jesus' teaching of the crowd again in 11:27–30. Why did Matthew not signal this shift with a transition? It is hard to answer such a question. What we can see however is that Matthew's Jesus did not miss a beat, and the context shows that Jesus was once again addressing the crowd. The only answer we can come up with is that Matthew considered the prayer and the call to be intimately linked. Jesus thanked God for the elect in his prayer and then addressed those who were elect in the next breath. This brings us to the passage in question.

Jesus' teaching becomes clearer yet in 11:28–30. If we take into consideration all that has been said above, then the meaning of 11:28–30 becomes quite specific. Within the context of the chapter, Jesus had already given reasons why coming to him was necessary for the weary and burdened. First, it was because Jesus was the one John prepared for (11:4–19). Second, it was because rejection of Jesus would result in condemnation (11:20–24). Third, it was because the only way to God was through Jesus (11:25–27).

Jesus then described his rest as the easy and light yoke. What, in fact, does this mean? This is where interpretations often stray quite a bit from the specific meaning by generalizing and contextualizing too quickly to "our" lives. As we have stated above, if we consider the entire chapter 12 as the context, then Jesus' rest is easy to understand and his yoke, no doubt, becomes clear.

The first story in chapter 12 has to do with Sabbath. In Aramaic or Hebrew, "Sabbath" means "rest." Since Matthew's audience knew the connection, they must have known how the "rest" in 11:28–29 relates to the Sabbath story of chapter 12.

Jesus transformed the Sabbath by allowing his disciples to feed their hunger. Furthermore, he healed a crippled man in 12:9–14 on the Sabbath. The remaining passage shows the rejection of the Pharisees towards Jesus. In other words, chapter 12 is an illustration of the meaning of chapter 11. What then is the meaning of 11:28–30, if we are to summarize it? Jesus meant for "rest" to be a new respect for life (e.g., even something as small as eating in 12:1–2) over rigid Torah adherence. He was not against the Torah as much as he was for a new age. The new age inaugurated by the "Lord of Sabbath" (12:8) provided the transformation. The yoke of the Torah gave way to the yoke of the Son of Man.

Now that the meaning has become clear for 11:28–30, it is worth exploring its relationship with surrounding sermons in Matthew. In chapter ten, Jesus talked about the contrarian kingdom ministry of the twelve. The sermon talks about the kind of absolute commitment that would result in persecution and conflicts. Jesus once again used that special description of God as "my Father" to demonstrate his authority in 10:32. In the sermon of chapter 13, Jesus began by talking about the various receptions of the kingdom, in his first parable (13:3–23). Jesus then talked about the mixed characters in the kingdom (13:24–30). Jesus also talked about smallness and the great impact of the kingdom (13:31–33). Jesus further talked about the previously hidden treasure, which is like the kingdom (13:44–46). Finally, Jesus talked about separation and judgment within the kingdom at the final judgment (13:47–51).

There is a progressive theme about the kingdom that deserves our attention in chapter 13. From the first to the last parables in Matthew 13, the narrative plot progresses in this way: Jesus talked about receiving the kingdom right at the start, simply because the kingdom message had to be received in order for membership to take place (13:3–23). In the present time, it is difficult to assess who the weeds and wheat are, but the kingdom grows tremendously (13:24–33). It is because of its preciousness that Jesus did not want to uproot all the bad elements at this point, but there will be a day when separation between the good and the bad will happen (13:44–50).

In light of chapter 10, we can now summarize the meaning of 11:28–30. While chapter 10 emphasizes the hardship of the kingdom mission, 11:28–30 provides a balance by talking about the rest the citizens will find. The conflict that follows in chapter 12 shows the sources of hardship. In his definition of "rest," Jesus went directly against social-religious convention. This "rest" results in hardship. Thus, the tension is ironic. In finding the greatest rest, the disciples faced the greatest persecution.

We must understand this irony in light of the parables in Matthew 13. The parables give the progress of the kingdom, inaugurated by Jesus' first coming and culminated by his second coming. When Jesus used kingdom language, he was talking about the kingdom in Jewish terms that point towards Israel. The Jews wished for the restoration of YHWH's kingdom. Jesus used their language to communicate how the kingdom actually worked. Within Israel, there were weeds and wheat in the membership. Based on the discussion about those who came to Jesus for rest, the weeds were clearly those who aligned with people who persecuted Jesus but claimed to be religious members of Israel's kingdom (e.g., Pharisees). The persecutors would face future judgment.

We can now readily summarize the meaning of 11:28–30. Jesus' rest consists of a transformation of the present reality into a higher reality. He valued life more than rigid religious stipulations, but this value would draw a lot of persecution. The community Jesus envisioned was a life-saving community, and not a Sabbath-keeping, Pharisaic community. Israel was never meant to find rest in Sabbath keeping, according to Jesus. Instead, her ultimate purpose was to create a community that valued the life of each member, from top to bottom. Even facing persecution, the disciples were to live in this rest not as an escape but as a staunch stance against rigid adherence to the Torah without consideration of what God valued most: life. In healing and serving others like Jesus, the disciples would become missionaries of this rest, as more people come into it.

## APPLICATION

The application of 11:28–30, based on the above assessment, is more active than passive. The common misconception of a passive "rest" is utterly misguided. Jesus was not talking about a general escape from a believer's daily problems, but a specific transformation of the old order, in this case, the Sabbath, into the new order after the Messiah. A believer should not use his faith as an escape from life's problems. A prosperity focus for the gospel can mislead many. When Christians see Jesus' rest as a passive thing, an abnormal, otherworldly faith appears. It seems that rest can still happen when someone does something as mundane as feeding oneself. While living in Jesus' rest, the believer can be doing simple things or extraordinary things and she still lives in that rest.

Jesus was not a utopian who presented an illusion for his followers to escape. On the contrary, he challenged his follower to follow his hard path of valuing what God valued in serving and giving life to the community so that others may find rest. Having "rest" is not about appearing religious or respectable. Rather, it connotes a radical discipleship that is willing to challenge and break convention so that those who really need help may get help (e.g., the crippled man in chapter 12). By living along that path, the disciple receives true "rest" in the spirit of the Sabbath tradition and not just superficial keeping of the Sabbath. Instead of escaping from life's problems, Jesus teaches the Christian to solve such problems, not only for his own challenges but also for the society's challenges and injustices. Jesus advocates resting by helping others.

## MISTAKES TO AVOID

A common interpretive mistake is to cut out some saying from its context in order to apply it as evangelistic rhetoric. It may sound good, but it completely violates the message and gives the wrong impression of the gospel. In fact, in this case such a move gives the opposite meaning of the real message of the passage.

Another mistake interpreters often make is ignoring the wider book context. Any sermon that is connected to the occasion and location of a narrative automatically relates to that narrative. This is a hard and fast rule. The consideration of surrounding context really sheds more light on Jesus' saying. Any part of the book belongs with all the other parts. It is a mistake not to do this with great care in Matthew. I have only scratched the surface on this issue. I am sure my careful reader can continue this exercise until the entire context of Matthew will shed richer light still on 11:28–30. The final product is a strong biblical theology of Matthew.

## DISCUSSION QUESTIONS

- What is the problem with the popular interpretation of Matthew 11:28–30?
- What are some of the ways the "rest" can be interpreted based on surrounding narrative context?
- Look for other ways this idea of rest connects with other ideas in Matthew?
- Think about or discuss practical ways rest can take place in the Christian life, based on the above observations.

# 3

# Matthew 18— Church Discipline? Prayer Meetings?

"If your hand or your foot causes you to stumble, cut it off and throw it away...."
"For where two or three gather in my name, there am I with them...."

## THE POPULAR MEANING

"We should 'Matthew 18' the violator," said one church leader regarding a church discipline situation. I couldn't believe my ears. "Matthew 18" had become a verb! Many think that the whole of Matthew 18:1–9 is about church discipline.

In recent news, some city ordinances have had problems with Christian home groups and even home churches. In one instance, the city fined a home group for holding a Bible study due to the fact that the home was not zoned for a church. One defender of the home group practice actually cited Matthew 18:20 to say that this was a violation of his religious rights. Leaving aside the legal situation, citation of this verse often connects with either prayer meetings or church meetings. The popular meaning of Matthew 18 comes from 18:15–20. Some may even misquote 18:20 as a promise for prayer meetings. The interpretation goes something like this: Since Jesus promised that where two or three gather in his name he would dwell among them, should we not attend prayer meetings where more than two or three gather?

## WHERE DOES THE PASSAGE BEGIN?

The passage could be said to begin in several places. At the broadest, it may begin in 17:1. This passage is part of all the events that were taking place, as the phrase "at that time" in 18:1 indicates. The narrower context starts at 17:24, after Jesus and his disciples arrived in Capernaum. The topic there deals with payment of temple tax with a coin miraculously produced from inside a freshly caught fish. The two prior accounts deal with transfiguration (17:1–13) and the healing of a demonized boy (17:14–23).

The narrative that follows this sermon comes in 19:1—22:46. The story starts with a discussion on divorce (19:1–11), followed by Jesus' dealing with little children (19:12–15), and discussion about the rich young man (or any rich man for that matter) entering the kingdom (19:16–30), aptly illustrated by the parable about vineyard workers, where the last will come first (20:1–16). The rest of the narrative leads Jesus to Jerusalem, starting with a prediction about his death (20:17–19), followed by a mother's request for her sons to reign with Jesus (20:20–28) and the healing of two blind men (20:29–34). Chapter 21 starts Passion Week, which leads to the next sermon starting in chapter 23.

Most certainly, 18:35 marks the end of the sermon, whether we take its beginning as 17:1 or 17:24. Especially important is the situation that prompted Jesus' talk in 18:1, where the disciples had a question about who was the greatest in the kingdom.

## THE MEANING OF THE PASSAGE

The passage seems to consist of four sections:

| 18:2–9 | discussion about the little ones |
|---|---|
| 18:10–14 | lost sheep parable |
| 18:15–20 | the brother who sins against someone |
| 18:21–35 | discussion on forgiveness through the parable of the unmerciful servant |

The discussion mainly talks about who is the greatest. The importance of the little child certainly received due attention (18:2–6). In fact, Jesus wanted to emphasize the importance by stressing the penalty of causing one of the little ones to stumble: death by drowning with a millstone (18:9). The offense is just as serious as other moral issues (e.g., 5:29). Though punishment is severe in this world, the eternal judgment is worse (18:6).

Having talked about the little ones, Jesus now used a parable of the lost sheep to illustrate in 18:10–14. If the parable values the lost sheep, it teaches that every little one counts. Based strictly on Jesus' context, the traditional evangelistic interpretation of this parable falls very much short of the mark. The parable is not about salvation as much as the value of the ones that are have wandered off, because the story illustrates the truth spoken in 18:1–9. In other words, these lost ones were originally in the right path but somehow went off it and need to be brought back by Jesus or the community of faith. Jesus exhorted his disciples to reverse their value system from the world's because during his time, children were not viewed with high regard. The kingdom exists for the sake of the little ones and not the other way around. Even Christ the King identifies with the children in 18:5. Status in the kingdom is often inversely proportional to status in the world.

In relation to the little one is the erring brother, to whom Jesus turns his attention in 18:15–19. This is not a standalone paragraph because Jesus had not stopped talking nor switched location from 18:14. After dealing with the problem of stumbling in 18:2–9, Jesus dealt with the problem of confrontation and restoration of the offensive person who had stumbled. Here Jesus dealt with the other side of the issue about offending someone. In 18:15, the offended, and not the offender, takes responsibility for the first step of restoration. True forgiveness is not a matter of avoidance, but of confronting and resolving problems between people. Jesus was not saying to forgive and forget but rather to confront and resolve. The offended should confront rather than avoid the pain. The two-witness requirement is in line with Deuteronomy 17:6–7 and Matthew 19:15. The previous context prevents stumbling. Here we deal with life after stumbling. Curiously, the word "church" occurs here in 18:17, with its only other occurrence in the entire book of Matthew being in 16.18. Since the church had not yet been established, Jesus used "church" in its simple meaning of Israelite assembly (i.e., synagogue). Jesus used similar vocabulary in 16:19 and 18:18 to draw a parallel between the authority of the church and that which was originally granted to Peter. Moreover, this whole process was to take place in a religious community. Jesus did not just say "two or three come together" but "*where* two or three come together." The "where" is vital.

The section of 18:19–20 is most commonly misunderstood. Many have taken this to be a promise of Jesus about public prayer meetings. This is absolutely wrong. Jesus intended the two or three people who gather to denote the same two or three witnesses from 18:16. In other words, this is a warning to those who were prepared to confront the erring brother. Jesus was saying that the steps that lead to discipline must be done in community through prayer.

Jesus wrapped up the entire discussion with a concluding parable about the merciless person, in 18:21–35. The moral of this parable is nothing unusual. It merely shows that the forgiveness received is in direct proportion to forgiveness granted. Mercy is at the forefront of dealing with erring brothers or the little ones. Forgiveness is part of the process when repentance happens. Jesus' focus was not on punishment, but restoration and forgiveness. This means that so long as the person is repentant, forgiveness is available—just like for tax collectors and gentiles. Gentiles and tax collectors are not role models (see 5:46–47) but can be recipients of salvation also (8:5–13; 9:9–13). The same word for "mercy" in 18:33 describes what Jesus did with Matthew in 9:13. Matthew was an outsider of Israel who responded to Jesus' call to follow him. So ultimately, the purpose of discipline in the community is repentance and restoration, not expulsion.

We have already dealt with the entire chapter and its relationship with other parts of Matthew. We must now focus more on the previous and subsequent context as to how the chapter fits. In so doing, we will find out its meaning in its fullest sense.

The whole idea of greatness presupposes the context of 17:24–27, where Jesus said that these disciples were great because they were identified with Jesus, who was the son of the "king." Who then is the greatest, besides Jesus? The disciples now asked the logical question. So far, the greatest was not measured in size or social status, but in terms of needs. The small child had a need for someone to watch out for so that he did not stumble. The erring brother had the need to rectify his action so that he could restore broken relationships. Jesus demonstrated his concern for the little ones by embracing the little children in 19:12–15. Jesus also showed definitively that status played no part in greatness when he discussed the situation of the rich young man (or any rich man) in 19:16–30. This was only confirmed by the parable of the vineyard workers. The last came in first because greatness was not measured by accomplishment (20:1–16).

In summary, Matthew was not only concerned with showing the counterculural kingdom value of greatness (or smallness). He was also keen to emphasize what was "not" greatness. Although the question in 18:1

that started the entire discussion has to do with the greatest in the kingdom, Jesus turned the topic upside down by talking about the smallest in the kingdom. Such is the logic of the kingdom. This upside-down world was also to become the norm of Matthew's faith community.

## APPLICATION

As we have demonstrated above, Matthew 18 is not at all about a call for salvation (e.g., lost sheep) or church discipline (e.g., erring brother). Rather, it focuses on one overarching issue: Who is great? According to what Jesus had just said, we have to ask one question, "Who matters?"

Jesus demonstrated through this sermon that the kingdom where he ruled was contrary to the ones ruled by earthly values. It existed not for the strong but for the weak. Although the strong were not unwelcome, Jesus' care was especially for the weak—not only those outside of the faith community but also those inside of it.

The church can fall into one of two extremes. She either fails to cast any moral judgment, especially against the powerful, or she becomes overly judgmental. Both extremes are checked by the relational dynamics in this passage. Moral judgment is badly needed for a just community. Strong intellectual and prayerful wisdom are needed to make such a judgment. At the same time, the gracious relationship principle should guide the practice of this judgment so that the community can work together towards a greater cause without being hindered by immorality, on the one hand, or a harsh attitude on the other. The church should be both moral and gracious.

## MISTAKES TO AVOID

The vital mistake to avoid is the separation of sections of Jesus' sermon without considering the meaning of the whole. Each section is no doubt meaningful, but the whole is greater than the sum of its parts. The sermon should be considered as a linear speech with a starting and ending point. The beginning is the situation from which Jesus' sermon was spoken. Without understanding that Jesus was dealing with the question of greatness, much of our interpretation of this passage will fall apart. Everything in the same sermon should somehow point back to the issue Jesus was dealing with at the beginning.

Another mistake to avoid is the failure to connect sermon and narrative, especially with Matthew (and also John in later study). As we have seen, the narratives surrounding sermons are meaningful in helping illustrate the themes within the sermons. Neglect of the surrounding situation will limit our understanding of the passage itself.

## DISCUSSION QUESTIONS

- What are the problems of popular interpretations of Matthew 18?
- What is the main issue raised about discipline in the church community?
- What are the roles of the offender and offended in the process of restoration?
- How is the place where the two or three gather significant?
- How will we practically accomplish both righteousness and grace?

# 4

# Mark 6:14–29— A Gruesome Murder Only?

King Herod heard about this, for Jesus' name had become well known. Some were saying, "John the Baptist has been raised from the dead, and that is why miraculous powers are at work in him."
Others said, "He is Elijah."
And still others claimed, "He is a prophet, like one of the prophets of long ago."
But when Herod heard this, he said, "John, whom I beheaded, has been raised from the dead! ..."

## THE POPULAR MEANING

IF YOU GREW UP in Sunday school like I did, this story was probably not often told, due to its violent nature. The story could well be called "How John lost his head." The fact is that most people read it for the beheading of John the Baptist. What really is the point of such a violent story? It is very hard to comprehend, as it appears Mark stuck it in haphazardly here. Or did he?

## WHERE DOES THE PASSAGE BEGIN?

The passage seems to begin at Mark 6:14, according to popular divisions of many English translations. Yet, this beginning seems very abrupt with Herod Antipas hearing about something regarding Jesus, or whatever events, without clear reference to the specific stories he heard. No one tells a story with such a strange beginning. As we shall see, the passage ought to begin at 6:6b, where certain events took place, giving the Herod story a good beginning, but we are jumping ahead too quickly.

## THE MEANING OF THE PASSAGE

The story in 6:14–29 seems very puzzling because it surely could occur anywhere in Mark, especially the section right after 1:14. Somewhere between the imprisonment of John in 1:14 and here in chapter 6, John was executed. Mark gave no chronological indicator. This story in Mark 6 recounts what led up to John's execution. The placement of this story does not make any chronological sense at all here, unless we consider closely what Mark was trying to do. John, of all people, was the preparer for the way of the Lord in 1:1–8. In all the Gospels, John was intimately associated with the way of Jesus and the gospel. Most certainly, the beheading of John had something to do with the danger associated with doing the work of God's kingdom, whether the work was done by the Old Testament prophets, John the Baptist, Jesus, or Jesus' disciples. The narrative of John's execution serves as an apt illustration of danger, in this case for the preparer of the way of the Lord.

John preached the baptism of repentance in 1:4. Repentance was only needed when sins were involved (1:5). In the case of 6:17–18, Herod Antipas's marriage was sinful (cf. Leviticus 18:16; 20:21). The passage then implies that John confronted Herod about his sin. The passage shows Herodias to be the main perpetrator against John (6:19). Between Herodias and her husband, she was probably the most displeased with John because at least, we are told, Herod liked listening to John (6:20). When reading the problem of this story so far, Mark portrayed Herod and his family to be against the way John preached. They were, then, the kingdom's enemies.

How did John eventually die? The section of 6:21–28 blames Herod's wife Herodias, and her daughter. Apparently, Herodias had a deadly grudge against John all along (Mark 6:19). This occasion of the banquet became the "opportunity" in 6:21. The phrase in Greek for "opportunity" literally means "a good opportunistic day." It is a good opportunity because Herodias had harbored hatred towards John for a long time. Now was the chance to carry out her bitterness. Even the opportunity was an accident. This is the plot line:

| 6:21–22 | Herodias's daughter's dance |
| 6:23 | Herod promised her up to half of his kingdom |
| 6:24–25 | Herodias's suggestion to behead John |
| 6:26–28 | Herod's reluctant beheading of John |

This bloody story shows the kingdom messenger's death. Although John paved the way of the Lord, his confrontation with the earthly kingdom resulted in his life being cut short. The earthly kingdom seems to be winning. Yet, in order to understand the purpose of this gruesome story, we have to look at how this story began in Mark 6:14–16, and see that the placement of this story is not really about John's beheading. Mark only used the occasion to place a story from one of his sources about John's death here, but he had reasons for doing so.

The story right before the beheading was about the disciples' work after Jesus sent them out. If we read 6:14, Herod "heard" but the question is "What did he hear?" In context, the possibilities could be twofold: Jesus' work or the disciples' work. 6:12–13 seems to be talking about the disciples duplicating Jesus' work. Thus, the primary thing that Herod heard was likely the work of the disciples when they duplicated Jesus' ministry. The pattern Mark set up with the very concise description was that the disciples' ministry was a personification of Jesus' ministry. Due to the similar nature of ministry, they would also encounter the same kind of rejection and experience the same difficulty that all kingdom ministers experience (6:12–13). These disciples continued to walk in the way of the Lord. Thus, Herod heard about the disciples' work and thought that John the Baptist had arisen from the dead (6:14–16). This whole elaborate story, then, has its unexpected effect, in that it was not mainly about John at all. It is using John to illustrate two facts: the greatness of the disciples' work and the danger of kingdom work. Mark was careful to attribute such greatness to Jesus who delegated authority to his followers in 6:7.

What this particular passage has taught us is that not all divisions in our translations of the Bible are correct. Something as awkward as 6:14–29 has good explanation from previous context. Just by reading the story of John's beheading within the occasion from which the story arose can teach us a whole lot about the story's real power. In other words, the story of the disciples' mission and John's beheading ought to be viewed as one unit simply because 6:14 does not start a new section. The beginning of 6:14 records

Right Texts, Wrong Meanings

the main reason why Mark included this story. It gives an explanation as to what Herod had heard and the extent of the great work done by the disciples in 6:12–13. The long excursus about John only highlights the great impact John had in Herod's court being transferred to the great impact of the disciples' ministry.

## APPLICATION

What does the beheading story teach about discipleship? The story is about two different realities related to discipleship. First, it is about the danger of being a disciple. Since there were many smaller movements in Judaism during Jesus' time, why would the disciples or the way of Jesus the messiah be dangerous? Is it not because the entire movement was noticeable? The radical movement of Jesus and his followers was so noticeable that they were placed in great danger. Their impact moved beyond their own Jewish community into the imperial world. John the Baptist's fate was just a sample of the price they might have to pay. The picture portrays the kind of faith shown by both John and Jesus to go beyond indigenous Jewish religion into something with external impact. The very same can be said about modern discipleship.

The second reality of discipleship was that it had so much societal impact that even kings noticed. Discipleship is not something one does behind closed doors. It does not stop at personal piety or spirituality. Rather, it was a public event for Jesus' followers because they were personifying the work of Jesus through exorcism, healing, and preaching. Only when they personified Jesus' public work would they get the attention of those who did not normally pay attention to such religious matters. The disciples' work must have had great societal implications for Herod to mistake it for the resurrected John! Private spirituality in either ancient or modern faith will never have that kind of public impact. Each church community needs to face the same question. Does the society notice the ministry? Does the community have such a powerful impact that someone would mistake the work to be a resurrected person's?

One final point of application needs to be made about this story. We notice that Herod's confusion was about Jesus mainly. Was Jesus the resurrected John? Yet, the story prior is about the disciples' work. What point was Mark making? Mark was basically saying that the disciples' work had represented Jesus' work. The work of discipleship is draw people to Jesus, and not merely to the community itself. That, too, is the challenge facing the church in every age.

## MISTAKES TO AVOID

When dealing with a passage like Mark 6:14–29, it is quite easy to think that the content is the message. The content could contain part of the message, but the content is not the entire message. What we need to keep in mind are the details at the beginning, and ask "What exactly did Herod hear?" Within context, he heard about the disciples.

Upon seeing the disciples' work impacting Herod, we have to look broader still for the overall meaning of how this particular story about the beheading fits the overall narrative so far. Without seeing how one piece fits the puzzle, we will miss the point about the difficulty of being a servant to the kingdom. We may only surmise that this was just one more unfortunate incident recorded by the Bible, with no ethical implication.

## DISCUSSION QUESTIONS

- What is wrong with the popular understanding of John's beheading?
- How does the hearing of Herod relate to the previous story?
- How does this story find its place in the kingdom story Mark was trying to tell?
- What ethical implications does this story have for the modern reader?

# 5

# Mark 11:22–25—
# Prayers that Move Mountains?

"Have faith in God," Jesus answered. "Truly I tell you, if anyone says to this mountain, 'Go, throw yourself into the sea,' and does not doubt in their heart but believes that what they say will happen, it will be done for them. Therefore I tell you, whatever you ask for in prayer, believe that you have received it, and it will be yours. And when you stand praying, if you hold anything against anyone, forgive them, so that your Father in heaven may forgive you your sins."

### THE POPULAR MEANING

"Prayers that move mountains" have become a kind of cliché for powerful (and even magical) prayers. Last time I checked Amazon's catalog, around a dozen or more products use this cliché for titles. Do prayers move mountains? This is a huge question.

Mark 11:22–25 seems to be the exact passage we need in order to answer the question at hand. However, we shall see that the mountainous prayer is overrated, at least in the message Mark was trying to convey.

### WHERE DOES THE PASSAGE BEGIN?

The passage is part of a greater narrative. It naturally begins at 11:20 because the narrator gives the occasion and location of the event. It is also important to deal with a broader narrative that precedes this story, because the story of the fig tree that contains this saying is itself part of the narrative about Jesus' clearing of the temple.

## THE MEANING OF THE PASSAGE

Let us plot out this story in the greater scheme of things in Mark. Jesus came into Jerusalem in 11:1-11 and received a warm welcome. Jesus then cursed a fig tree in 11:12-14 and then cleared the temple in 11:15-18. The next day, Jesus came by to see the fig tree and taught the disciples about prayer in 11:20-25. The outline looks like this:

| 11:1-11 | triumphal entry into Jerusalem |
|---|---|
| 11:12-14 | cursing of the fig tree |
| 11:15-18 | clearing of the temple |
| 11:20-21 | discovering of the dead fig tree |
| 11:22-25 | teaching about prayer |

These stories are all related because the plot starts and ends with the tree. However it is a very puzzling series of stories, not just the part about prayer level, but the entire plot about the fig tree.

The puzzle starts with 11:12-14. The problem the narrator presents is Jesus' hunger in 11:12. The fig tree did not solve Jesus' problem when Jesus looked for something to eat. The narrator adds the curious fact that it was because it was not the season for figs. However, Jesus did expect fruits even if it seemed unreasonable. Thereafter, Jesus cursed the tree in 11:14. The negative language is especially emphatic in the Greek. We can translate it as, "May no one ever eat fruits from you for good." This was the only phrase Jesus uttered in the entire fig episode in 11:12-14. The phrase highlights the importance of Jesus' curse as being decisive and final. We shall see that Jesus' curse acts as a parable to the subsequent episode in the temple.

Jesus then entered the temple and drove out all the moneychangers and all those who did the buying and selling in the temple court. Included were those selling doves, presumably a sacrifice for the poor (Leviticus 14:30). The inclusion of this bird gives a hint as to why Jesus would do such a thing. Jesus threw out these merchants because the temple was used to take advantage of the poor and had become a place of business. Since the temple had become an oppressive institution, Jesus called it a "den of robbers" in 11:17. Jesus' statement, though harsh, is not without ironic humor. The Jews considered Romans the robbers of their land. Yet, Jesus here called the religious institution a den of robbers. Jesus was surely making a point about what was wrong with the religious institution of his day. Jesus quoted Isaiah 56:7 in 11:17. The context of Isaiah 56 is about how Israel's temple should become a shining example to the nations. Clearly, that would have been the right thing to do. Jesus' point from the fig tree seems to make more sense if we read it in the context of the Isaiah passage.

The fig tree was clearly not in season. Analogically, the temple was also not in season to do what it was supposed to do, even though Isaiah clearly stated the function of the temple. With the gentiles surrounding the temple complex with the Antonia fortress, Jesus' day was the perfect time to use the temple to attract onlooking gentiles. Yet, Jesus expected fruit from both. Since no fruit was forthcoming from either, in season or not, they both received condemnation. The difference was that the fig tree was not supposed to be in season, whereas the temple was supposed to be in season based on Isaiah. It was precisely the failure of Israel's religion that caused the first exile.

There is a logical sequence to Jesus' action and speech. To Jesus, as he quoted Isaiah 56, Israel was once again in exile. Therefore, if a fig tree that was not in season received a curse, how much greater of a curse would the temple receive? This seems to be what Jesus was saying. By pronouncing a curse on the fig tree first and then clearing the temple, Jesus was making an argument from lesser to greater to teach a lesson. The condemnation of the temple was a foregone conclusion. Now we have finally arrived at the passage in question.

The next day, the disciples were passing through to see the fig tree again, apparently going to the temple with Jesus, and saw the fig tree dead (11:20–21). No one knew when it died. Jesus then made some puzzling hyperbolic statements in 11:22–25 that do not seem to relate at all to the temple. The present account seems puzzling. If we put Jesus back into his geographical context, the whole hyperbole about the mountain is easy to understand. Jesus was just near Jerusalem. The mountain there could well be the temple mount. "This" mountain may be that specific mountain on which the temple sat. The sea where the mountain would go was probably the Mediterranean Sea. Perhaps, the hyperbole indicates that at some future date when the temple would be destroyed, Jesus' teaching would make sense. In the same way of believing Jesus' prophecy, the faith community could also pray with the same faith.

It may seem that Jesus was extending the fig story too far, but the careful reader will note that Jesus was continuing his discussion of prayer from 11:17. This teaching on prayer is not merely a general abstraction. It is in relation to the prayerful function of the temple. If the temple was cursed, where would the house of prayer be? Jesus used the opportunity to relate this to prayer because the discipleship community would become the future house of prayer.

Jesus was talking about prayer to prepare his followers for the future. Soon, he would die and the disciples would be left alone. Furthermore, we have to get the meaning of the author Mark as well in the way he blended these stories together. These stories only seem loosely related but under Mark's artistry, they blend theologically (more precisely, eschatologically). Mark was using the event to cast a side-glance at the future of the temple. Knowing Jesus' prophecy would come to pass, the community must trust in the faithful Lord and become the new Israel where the temple failed. Jesus talked about two principles of prayer in 11:22–25: faith and reconciliation. Faith and reconciliation will characterize the new Israel and new community.

What kind of community would the disciples become? Jesus was very clear in 11:24–25. The community would be one of faith and reconciliation. A praying community can cause something as monumental as the removal of the temple mount. Mark's audience would be quite familiar with the image already.

## APPLICATION

As we have seen, the above discussion moves way beyond an abstract idea of powerful prayer that moves abstract (or worse yet, metaphorical) mountains. It is part of the trend Jesus had set up to discuss the fate of the temple and his followers' future. This theme becomes even clearer in Mark 13. For now, Jesus wanted his disciples to know that the religious institution of Israel should be about a few basic things: prayer, faith, and reconciliation. Since the present religious institution could not accomplish those simple things, Jesus pronounced judgment upon it.

Jesus' teaching illuminates today's church. Modern church often looks more like the business of the temple with the goal that "bigger is better."

The focus on finance and architectural hardware of church growth can be overwhelming. Jesus' teaching reminds believers that the Christian faith is really about very few basic things. The rest is not the main dish. They are supporting sides. When the sides become the main entrée, the faith will fall under a curse.

## MISTAKES TO AVOID

The popular meaning has its own difficulty but has a few things to commend it. The teaching was in part about prayer, but it is much more. All the discussion about the mountain and sea does not make sense unless we take into consideration the geographical location and the surrounding stories. Sure, Jesus was being hyperbolic, but his image was based on a visible reality.

The prayer link is legitimate but will only make sense when we link it with the temple as a prayer house. It is therefore dangerous for us to directly apply the entire teaching into our present situation, instead of seeking answers from the surrounding texts.

## DISCUSSION QUESTIONS

- Besides prayer, what else could Jesus be talking about in this passage?
- How does the death of the fig tree fit into Jesus' teaching about the temple?
- How does the story illustrate what would happen later?
- How can this story inform our modern faith?

# 6

# Luke 2:1–20—
# The "Humble" Baby Jesus?

And there were shepherds living out in the fields nearby, keeping watch over their flocks at night. An angel of the Lord appeared to them, and the glory of the Lord shone around them, and they were terrified. But the angel said to them, "Do not be afraid. I bring you good news that will cause great joy for all the people. Today in the town of David a Savior has been born to you; he is the Messiah, the Lord. This will be a sign to you: You will find a baby wrapped in cloths and lying in a manger. . . ."

### THE POPULAR MEANING

THE POVERTY AND HUMILITY of Jesus has become standard fare in Sunday school. This passage contributes. The popular meaning of this passage is quite simple. I have heard it often during Christmas time. It goes something like this: Baby Jesus came in a manger as a humble human being. So we should all be humble like him and reflect on how much he has sacrificed for us. Certainly, this may be good theology or a sentimental advent story, but none of this is exactly from the text.

## WHERE DOES THE PASSAGE BEGIN?

The passage begins at 2:1. There is little doubt about Luke's presentation as he finished with the story about John the Baptist and now moves on to Jesus. It is possible to finish the story at 2:20, but it is also possible to link it to the presentation at the temple. For now, we can limit the passage to 2:1–20.

## THE MEANING OF THE PASSAGE

Right at the birth of Jesus, the shepherds were the first ones to find him in 2:8–21. This fact has huge implications. The occasion was the census given by Augustus (2:1). Jesus' movement seems to have been controlled by imperial forces. The exaggerated claim of Augustus's census for "all the Roman world" is a significant literary device (2:1; cf. Acts 1:8), showing imperial geography that was firmly recognized in the audience's world.[1] The story also raises the question of who the real king is. Was Jesus or Augustus the lord of the world and savior of his people? This story might give some hints about who would be king. Why would there be kingly implications? The discussion of king David would be the strongest road sign (1:69, 74; 2:4, 11).

At this stage, we should note that the shepherds were out in the countryside. They were not moving around due to the census because they did not belong to the mainstream. Their work did not allow them to be steadily in one place because of the sheep's grazing habits. Their profession kept them out of imperial control, and Bethlehem had grass at the moment. Their location allowed them to find baby Jesus, but things were not that simple.

The first part in 2:1–7, especially 2:7, shows that Jesus had no place to lay his head because the inn was full. If the story ended there, we may well say that Jesus was there in humble surroundings, and that he came as a humble and rejected baby. This could well be the meaning without the shepherds, but Luke focused the entire plot on the shepherds and not merely the humble birth. The humble birth was the introduction to the story and not the ending or the climax of the story. The immediate story about the shepherds would soon show why exactly Jesus had to be born in the manger. The popular notion of his humble birth, when we connect the birth story with the preparation for the shepherd's meeting, will be proven inadequate. We must turn out attention to the material Luke was interested in.

---

1. For the purpose of this study, we assume the same author for Luke and Acts.

*Luke 2:1–20—The "Humble" Baby Jesus?*

The appearance of angels, like the other appearances so far in 1:11, 26 denotes God's revelation. The content of the angel's proclamation further shows the location as being divinely controlled and not under the control of the imperial census. The angels told the shepherds that the baby in a manger would be a sign to the shepherds in 2:12. Luke's description in 2:12 matched exactly the description in 2:7. In other words, the manner of Jesus' birth was precisely a sign to the shepherds. What is so special about this sign?

First, if the inn had room, then, Jesus would have had place to lay his head within a good room and the shepherds would not have found him without knocking on every room in every inn in Bethlehem.[2]

Second, the sign is significant. Normally, the word "sign" identifies an event or person of significance. Certain people or events ought to qualify as signs in the stories leading to Jesus' birth, but Luke refrained from using that term. For example, when Zechariah took a long time and became dumb, the people saw his dumbness as an indicator that something special had happened in 1:21–22. Yet, Luke did not use "sign" to describe what clearly looked like a sign to the people. Then, Elizabeth was pregnant and it became a sign to Mary according to Gabriel the angel in 1:36. At least the pregnancy qualified as a sign. Yet, Luke again did not use the word "sign" to describe it until the manger birth of Jesus.

The manger was a special place because Luke called it a sign. The event was a special event for a special group of people. The shepherds' astonishment in 2:18 was also a confirmation of their special place in seeing God's special work because word "astonish" was also used of the Pentecost miracle and the healing of the lame man in Acts 2:7 and Acts 4:13. In Luke, astonishment was the normal reaction towards something extraordinary and divine (e.g., Luke 8:25; 11:14). Not only was Jesus special, but the way God located him to be found by the shepherds was even more special. That's Luke's assessment.

Although the shepherds were the first to witness Jesus, they remain nameless. They were outsiders to the society where they plied their trade,

---

2. Scholars have debated as to what the "inn" actually means. The Greek word for "inn" usually just means "house." Some see it as a small house. Others see it as possibly and quite specifically a house owned by Joseph or one of his relatives in his hometown Bethlahem. It is definitely possible that they had stayed in such a small place that Mary could not spread out for the childbirth procedure. Thus, they were relegated to using the attached stable with a manger. Perhaps the focus is not on whether the "inn" was full of people like it is some kind of Hilton Hotel.

mostly outside of the city limits. They got the front seat to watch God's work take place right in the humble manger at an inn. The special point of this passage is not merely the manger. We need to probe further through the plot. The manger's special purpose was the special point that God's heart was to reveal himself through Jesus the Savior to those in the fringe (e.g., 4:18–19). This story sets the trend for the rest of Jesus' ministry in the Gospel. The kingdom was made up of people such as these. Earthly kingdoms, such as that of Caesar's, were all about riches, whereas Jesus' kingdom focused on those excluded by earthly kingdoms.

## APPLICATION

The application of this passage is quite practical. It is not meant to evoke an emotional response about the humility of Jesus. Other passages can do that. Rather, the story is to show that Christmas was the gospel to the poor. The church needs to bring a gospel to the poor that does not only satisfy their material needs, but to also shows them who the real Jesus Christ is.

In the past, the church has struggled when it comes to the poor. The social gospel advocates merely provide the poor with material supply, thinking that they are doing the Lord's will. Many evangelical churches that reject the social gospel have grown into upwardly mobile, middle class churches. Such comfortable churches merely preach the gospel through words to the poor while emphasizing the "spiritual" need of all people whether rich or poor. Both sides have rejected what is essential. The poor need both material and immaterial aspects of the gospel. Material goods can help them fill their needs, but they are not enough. Preaching the gospel verbally can help them understand the gospel logically and intellectually, but that is also not enough. Both are necessary. Both can be done in Christ's name. That seems to be the application for Luke's Christmas account.

## MISTAKES TO AVOID

The mistake to avoid is failing to consider the surrounding context of Jesus' birth narrative. Instead, many misinformed interpreters have taken it for granted that a lot of popular interpretations of the birth story are right. Yet, as is usually the case, a story has its meaning in surrounding contexts. In fact, the whole idea of poverty can also show up in the next story about Jesus' presentation in temple when his parents offered a poor man's sacrifice in 2:24 (cf. Leviticus 12:8). The theme continues if the interpreter looks carefully at these stories, not by themselves, but within the larger framework of Luke's narrative world.

## DISCUSSION QUESTIONS

- What is wrong with the sentimental birth interpretation?
- How is the usage of the word "sign" helpful in understanding this passage?
- How does the social status of the shepherds impact the interpretation of this story?
- How will the church express the spirit of Jesus' birth in ministry?

# 7

# Luke 6:17–26— Poverty as the Ultimate Good?

"Blessed are you who are poor, for yours is the kingdom of God. Blessed are you who hunger now, for you will be satisfied. Blessed are you who weep now, for you will laugh. Blessed are you when people hate you, when they exclude you and insult you and reject your name as evil, because of the Son of Man.

"Rejoice in that day and leap for joy, because great is your reward in heaven. For that is how their ancestors treated the prophets.

"But woe to you who are rich, for you have already received your comfort. Woe to you who are well fed now, for you will go hungry. Woe to you who laugh now, for you will mourn and weep. Woe to you when everyone speaks well of you, for that is how their ancestors treated the false prophets.

## THE POPULAR MEANING

IN THE ROMAN CATHOLIC tradition, the vow of poverty is a serious issue. It has been interpreted and practiced by various orders. Some have even gone as far as to see poverty as a virtue. Can Luke 6:17–26 be viewed as reliable biblical evidence in favor of poverty?

This part of Luke is popularly known as the "Sermon on the Plain" in relation to the "Sermon on the Mount" of Matthew 5–7. The popular approach to this section is to harmonize it with Matthew 5:3–10, except that in the Matthew passage there are more beatitudes than in Luke 6.

*Luke 6:17–26—Poverty as the Ultimate Good?*

Due to the differences, some have concluded that Luke edited out some material from Matthew. Others see these as two different sermons. Certainly, there are reasons why people see the parallels between Matthew and Luke. After all, both passages use the beatitudes to begin Jesus' sermon.

Many popular interpreters also like to make a big deal out of this passage because it talks much about poverty and material wealth. Indeed, this appears to be the central content of the passage. There seems to be much about advocating poverty over wealth, or is there? The answer to the question once again should come from Luke's context.

## WHERE DOES THE PASSAGE BEGIN?

The passage begins exactly at 6:17. In Luke, the context is the selection of Jesus' twelve apostles in 6:12–16. This passage then begins as the first sermon Jesus preached to the twelve after their selection.

It is equally important to ask where this passage ends. It ends at 6:49. We can see a lot of abbreviations of what appears to be the Sermon on the Mount from Matthew 5–7, except there are parts from Matthew 5–7 that appear elsewhere in Luke's Gospel. How Luke edited this material, or whether Jesus taught these things multiple times, we will never know. The best approach is to take 6:17–26 as part of the larger sermon Jesus taught in 6:17–49.

It will be helpful to see the subsequent topics within this sermon, in order to better appreciate Luke 6:17–26. Following 6:26, Jesus taught about love and mercy to enemies in 6:27–36. Thereafter, Jesus taught about judging others in 6:37–42. Traditionally, people divide the passage at 6:43, but there appears to be continuity to Jesus' teaching all the way to the end in 6:43–49. There is in fact, great deal of continuity from Jesus' teachings even starting from 6:27. We must then try to gain meaning from the whole rather than treating the parts as unrelated.

What is the meaning as the whole? We must divide the whole into two opposing topics with a conclusion. The outline is as follows:

| 6:27–36 | love for enemies |
| 6:37–45 | judging brothers |
| 6:46–49 | reverence for Jesus' lordship and fruit bearing |

## THE MEANING OF THE PASSAGE

Luke 6:20 is the key to understanding this passage. Jesus directed his remark to the disciples (plural) as a group with the repeated "you" also in plural. Those who hear in 6:27 continue to be the same group of disciples. Some popular preachers, especially those with the intention to influence social reform (not that social reform through the church is bad), misunderstand that this passage addresses the poor in general. We must let the plurals be our guide in seeing the audience to be disciples as a group, not as individuals. In other words, Jesus was talking about one kind of people over against other kinds of people. The "other" kind contains the people of woe. Thus, the entire function of the passage is to show the difference between those who followed Jesus, in this case, the disciples, and those who did not.

There is one common theme running through 6:17–23: poverty. Along with this poverty comes suffering and persecution. Luke 6:23 provides the transition to the section of woes, as it talks about the reward in heaven. Thus, in the light of the selection of the twelve disciples, Jesus encouraged them to suffer for the sake of the Son of Man so that they would receive their rewards.

Yet, based on the above discussion, the section of 6:24–26 contains four woes in contrast to the four beatitudes of the previous section. In other words, if the previous section of beatitudes describes the normal characteristics of the disciples, then the following section of woes describes abnormal characteristics. In other words, if we look closely at the emphasis on the Son of Man in the previous section, Jesus was not merely denouncing wealth or comfort in the woes, but denounced such gain due to compromise. Especially pronounced is 6:26, where he compared the kingdom enemies to false prophets. In other words, the poor people Jesus referred to were the ones who refused to get rich through compromise of kingdom principles.

Before we understand how wealth compromised kingdom principles in Jesus' time, we must gain a brief understanding of the nature of wealth in ancient society. Unlike today where some Western governments provide aid (though probably inadequately) to the poor, food problems were always financial problems, for most of the land ownership and money were in the hands of the wealthy minority. In that period, there was almost no middle class. This is an important point to note, because the people of the Roman Empire depended entirely on good economics in order to have something to eat. Food riots were not uncommon in various cities in the empire. Lack

## Luke 6:17–26—Poverty as the Ultimate Good?

of food could lead to instability. Food shortage could well indicate mismanagement of the area or that the gods had been angry with the empire. Abundance of food, however, would cause many to experience contentment. The provider of food then would gain honor and accolade from both the emperor and the people.

Upper class Jews gained from this system and bought up land. Severe oppression started here. The massive majority of landownership fell into the hands of a few. The landowners owned the food. Those who owned the food owned the people. Those with money could make high interest loans to those who had little. The vicious cycles continued. The only way to gain more wealth was to participate in this cycle. In simple terms, the rich ran the system and the poor sat under its oppression. If we keep in mind this background of wealth in the first century, the ethical interpretation of our present passage makes sense. Jesus was not mainly advocating for poverty or for the poor as much as for integrity.

The meaning of the passage can now extend to the rest of the sermon. I believe the beatitudes and woes set the foundation for the entire sermon. The first obstacle the disciples will encounter will be enemies. This is more than obvious because the previous passage talks about persecution. Of course, there will be enemies! Their enemies probably would cause even greater poverty to those who were kingdom citizens (i.e., Jesus' disciples). Some irresponsible evildoers could also contribute to such poverty (6:34). How then must the disciples treat the enemies? Jesus' reply was simple. They must treat the enemy with love to show the difference of being a kingdom citizen.

Jesus finally concluded by calling for his followers to set themselves on the firm foundation of his teachings, even if the result was persecution or poverty. What teaching, though? I would say the teaching, in this context, is about forgiving enemies (6:27–36) and being lenient towards a brother (6:37–45). This teaching is the firm foundation of discipleship.

Most people who look at either the beatitudes in general, or denouncement against wealth in particular, miss the point Jesus made in this speech. The speech was directed to the disciples for their faithfulness. It was an encouragement for them to remain faithful to be advocates of the Son of Man by bearing fruits that include love of enemies, tolerance of the erring brother, and quickness to do good works. It is easy to resent the enemy who has caused poverty and persecution in the first place, but Jesus called for love rather than hatred. In teaching this way, Jesus' focus was on relationships, and not material goods.

## APPLICATION

The application of such a passage is quite simple. We must first recognize that followers of Jesus function not only as individuals, but as a group. If all individuals will act out their faith towards each other, they will function well as a group. Jesus did not create individual believers only, but by joining them together, ultimately created a community. This community can be at odds with the outside world, which at times could attack it. Jesus showed the reason why the two are at odds. It is because the two kinds of people hold opposing values. Yet, the disciples were not to hate the opponents. Instead, they should love.

Logically, based on the suffering of the disciples, Jesus showed some of those kingdom values. First, he advocated loving of enemies who attacked the community. The progress of the kingdom is not through violence but through love. Second, he advocated careful judgment, instead of arbitrary and individualistic judgment, on all people a little later in 6:37–45, in order to assure proper ethics within the community. These are the baselines of the kingdom community. Jesus, finally, advocated for all citizens to carry out this firm foundation.

When looking at something like the above, the church has a strong responsibility today for its public witness. Often, no matter where the church stands politically, it can sound more judgmental than communal. Jesus was not advocating poverty as something good in and of itself, but was calling for a strong public showing of integrity. Churches can fall off the integrity wagon quite easily by misrepresenting the enemies within a hostile society. Somehow, they deem that the end justifies the means. Even if the enemies are wrong, however, the church that does not use the right means also is wrong. Jesus called for public engagement that most represents kingdom values.

## MISTAKES TO AVOID

The first mistake to avoid is the direct application of the passage "as is." Those who think the passage deals only with the poor are not careful readers of context. The passage directly addresses the disciples and must be treated in light of that. There is nothing blessed about being poor unless there is a reason for such poverty (i.e., discipleship). This, too, is a mistake of not taking the origin of such a passage seriously. While we may believe that God loves the poor and so should we, this passage cannot justify our belief. There are other more suitable passages from other parts of the Bible, especially parts of the Prophets, that give a more direct command to love and care for the poor.

The second mistake is to try to harmonize the beatitudes with Matthew's. Harmonization dulls the cutting edge of Jesus' sermon within Luke's story, and muddles the entire application. The form and function of the passage are both different than Matthew's. There is no reason to presuppose that the two can be harmonized into one. Matthew's does not have matching woes. Neither does Luke have as many beatitudes. Harmonization does no justice to the original meaning of such a passage.

The third mistake is to cut out parts of the same sermon to make each individual part meaningful apart from context. The sermon runs as one ongoing argumentation in the same way some clothing pieces are meant to fit together. Pulling it apart from context renders the passage meaningless much like mismatched clothing. Worse yet, the interpreter can make the passage mean whatever he wants it to mean when such dissection happens.

## DISCUSSION QUESTIONS

- What is wrong with seeing poverty as the main virtue in the passage?
- What is the cause of poverty from the passage?
- What virtue did Jesus teach his followers?
- What situations today are similar to those in Jesus' day in terms of poverty and integrity?

# 8

## Luke 10:38–42—
## Submissive Mary Against Fussy Martha?

As Jesus and his disciples were on their way, he came to a village where a woman named Martha opened her home to him. She had a sister called Mary, who sat at the Lord's feet listening to what he said. But Martha was distracted by all the preparations that had to be made. She came to him and asked, "Lord, don't you care that my sister has left me to do the work by myself? Tell her to help me!"

"Martha, Martha," the Lord answered, "you are worried and upset about many things, but few things are needed—or indeed only one. Mary has chosen what is better, and it will not be taken away from her."

### THE POPULAR MEANING

ONE OF THE MOST socially radical but often overlooked passages in the New Testament is Luke 10:38–42, where Martha is contrasted against her sister Mary. Academic interpreters tend to fall into two extremes of either saying that the passage has everything or nothing to do with women's societal roles.

In addition to the academic debate among scholars, our popular imagination tends to take this passage into all different directions. Quite often, leftover memory of Sunday school in a certain type of Christian context warps the interpretation of this story. As I search online, Mary and Martha jokes are in abundant. One writer asks, "Are you Mary or Martha?" Another jokes that Martha's way of cooking is to put an apple in the potatoes to keep them from budding, while Mary just buys the instant potato mix. The jokes go on and on. The first question makes the common mistake of too quickly identifying with biblical characters. The jokes make the mistake of comparing the busyness of Martha with the laziness of Mary.

Many who read this story cannot help but feel bad for Martha whose hard work had not only gone unnoticed, but even seems to have been condemned by Jesus. People can even say that Martha represents justification by works while Mary represents faith. Others see typology of two kinds of people with Martha being too busy serving and Mary being more focused on relationship with Jesus. Quite often popular interpretation imitates modern patriarchal stereotypes (i.e., nagging and fussing Martha, quiet and submissive Mary), but not first-century reality.

I keep using the term "popular" because this kind of moralizing interpretation is quite typical in our church communities. I suggest that we have gotten the meaning half-right at best. More often than not, the preacher completely misses the entire meaning. Nevertheless, the interpretation of this story within the popular imagination of modern preachers reflects more on their denominational and personal biases than a first-century context. What then did Luke mean in the way this passage is characterized?

## WHERE DOES THE PASSAGE BEGIN?

Usually, interpreters see the story beginning at 10:38, because of the change of location. However, if we look more broadly later, we must note that the story was part of the occasion of 10:25, due to thematic similarities. It was part of Jesus' discussion about the law with the teachers of the law. It was also part of what Jesus taught the disciples after his discussion with the teachers of the law. This division will prove to be important in our understanding. We are jumping ahead too fast at the moment, but we should first look closely at the event itself based on the location and occasion before we look at surrounding themes.

## THE MEANING OF THE PASSAGE

We must first look at the narrator's more obvious usage of vocabulary. The use of "preparations" which means "service" in Greek in Luke 10:40

describes Martha's work. The word "preparations" usually denotes service in a positive sense in Luke's writing (e.g., Acts 6:2, 4). Without a doubt, "service" was a positive description in the original Christian community. In fact, the Greek word for "service" gives birth to the original word for the office "deacon" in the early church. Some English translations tend to translate the "service" Martha differently than the usual positive usages elsewhere in the New Testament, but if we translate correctly, the ministries of Martha and other positive services are clearly connected here. I believe the deviation in translation reflects the interpretive biases of the translators, who miss the nuance of Luke's characterization. Martha's service would have been normally good in the social convention of those days, but she did not receive Jesus' compliment. Mary did! By sticking to the social convention of her day, Martha's expression received admonition instead of praise from Jesus.

Since avid readers of Luke tend to write books about female characters, there must be something about the gender question that is worth exploring. Luke, as is commonly noted, had extensive characterization about women in his writings. Now we can look at these characters from the point of view of female characters. It is important to explore the social reality of the first century to get a well-rounded understanding from the perspective of the original reader. Usually, the popular interpretation is that Mary had desired the heart of Jesus while Martha was too busy and that Jesus demanded a quiet spirit (sometimes even from a typological woman like Mary). Not that there is anything wrong with Mary desiring what was best in Jesus' eyes, but if we read the story in light of women's roles in the Roman household, we should gain a somewhat different perspective. There was nothing inherently bad about what Martha did because she received Jesus with hospitality as a friend of the kingdom, like other friends of the kingdom (cf. Luke 9:5; 10:8, 10). While the author used the narrator's voice to talk about Martha being distracted, Martha herself accused Mary of leaving her to do all the work. Thus, the narrative shows the accusation of Martha coming from a deeply rooted problem: she followed the social convention without considering her attitude in doing so. Her desire to follow the social convention had left her attitude unchecked. Martha was distracted by her service, but unthinkingly serving was the role of the woman in those days. Martha's task was not bad, but Mary had done better. Mary broke the convention, and Jesus gave her the compliment (Luke 10:41–42). Thus, through his association with the sisters, Jesus showed that the socially "good" could get "better."

Within Luke, the position of sitting "at the feet" suggests positional hierarchy (cf. Luke 7:36–50). More than likely, Mary acted as a guest while treating Jesus as the honored host or the Lord, but at the same time ready to help out in any way she can. Her position additionally shows her insight into Jesus' identity. For her, social convention was less important than a spiritual insight of Jesus as Lord. Thus, it is not a story about contemplation and meditation being better than active service, as some may be tempted to suggest.

Mary's action implicates much beyond her role modeling. She pointed to the messianic mission that would ultimately prioritize the words of the messiah symbolized by Mary's action over traditional societal conventions symbolized by Martha's action. She also taught a lesson about not being distracted by any kind of service, though service was no less important. In the story of the two sisters, the female role is the means by which Jesus taught a lesson for both men and women.

I think this story deserves to be read in the light of wider context of the chapter, especially in the light of the Samaritan story. I see the Samaritan story as one about a marginalized do-gooder who went all the way in serving another. He received a compliment from Jesus. In other words, the Martha story curbed the in- tensity of the Samaritan's story with a balance of heart with hard work. In other words, Luke used a woman's story not just so that he could teach about women's roles, but more importantly about lessons of attitude for the church beyond gender types. Both hospitality and the ministry of the word must be done with good attitude.

I believe the Mary and Martha story is there to provide a parallel with the Samaritan story, if we were to read both stories in terms of first-century social situation. Jesus continued to break boundaries by teaching Mary and letting her sit at his feet in 10:39. Luke artfully paired Martha's story with that of the good Samaritan's in Luke 10. Quite interestingly, the Samaritans were also marginalized. Luke was making comparison between the hard works of the good Samaritan and Martha, with one difference; Martha's work was met with disapproval. Jesus, then, was not merely pointing out that she was being too busy, but rather that she continued to be frazzled by her social convention. In other words, the Martha story curbed the in-tensity of the Samaritan's story with a balance of heart with hard work. In other words, Luke used a woman's story not just so that he could teach about women's roles, but more importantly about lessons of attitude for the church beyond gender types. Both hospitality and the ministry of the word must be done with good attitude.

Although many women followed Jesus, even in Luke's Gospel, we see the primary followers of Jesus to be men. Mary played a role reversal here. We may also contrast the two sisters. Martha was the protagonist of the story with her voice being heard throughout. Mary said nothing. Contrary to popular understanding, the story was more about Martha than about Mary, just based on the amount of material devoted to her. The very statistics on how many words were spoken between her and Jesus and how Jesus addresses her instead of Mary prove Martha to be the focus. Martha was the main character; Mary was only the object lesson. Martha however was the victim of, rather than victor over, the circumstances. Luke said that she was "distracted" by all the preparations. The verb "distracted" is in the Greek imperfect passive form, showing a continuous state (not just a moment of weakness) of being distracted as a victim of circumstances. Martha was working within her own social convention, thus causing her impatient outburst at her sister. We will soon compare Mary's situation with Martha's.

Within the story, Luke's description of Martha described perfectly the role of women in the Roman household. When reading this story, we can combine a sociological background with theology in reading it. Martha's work certainly fit social conventions because she worked hard like a good, little woman should in those days (Luke 10:40). An educated woman was as much of an oxymoron as a "good Samaritan" (cf. Luke 9:51–53; 10:25–37). As important as it is that Martha's story was socially revolutionary, the theme of Jesus' Messiahship is even more central to this passage and should not be missed.

Jesus was called the Lord there, the same title used for gentile rulers, including Caesar. Mary had not chosen what was better because she had stopped serving everyone. Mary had not chosen what was better because she did not work. She had chosen better because she recognized the same thing Luke recognized: Jesus as Lord. In so doing, she broke the social convention. She sat at the Lord's feet in a typical dining position, in contrast to Martha's busy service. Even if women were influential outside of the home (e.g., Lydia in Acts), they were usually defined by their household roles. Martha's labor typified women's roles both in Jewish and Roman society. That was her lot in life. On the contrary, Mary's role was anti-social in that typically, women were not known to be students. Men were. The popular interpretation of Mary accepting her role as quiet and submissive friend of Jesus needs a lot of correcting. She did the very opposite by breaking from tradition in her place as a disciple at Jesus' feet. Moreover, women were not to be present in meals in the same space as men unless they were courtesans. Yet, in this preparatory meal scene, Mary stayed at Jesus' feet as if she was ready to dine with him. She chose Jesus rather than the social conventions.

We can hardly get away from some discussion on gender simply because the story sets the women within their social role of functioning in private spaces (as opposed to public spaces). While women did not have the sort of legal rights they do today in our societies, they certainly had some access to the financial means of their male counterparts. Luke's record shows that many women of means had tried to use their resources to serve Christ's kingdom. Jesus (or more correctly Luke) used these women to teach a greater lesson beyond gender roles.

I think the meaning can be richer still, after all the discussions about context and gender. I put this out merely as an interpretive possibility my readers can think about. I may change my mind. I am merely suggesting a wider interpretation. I think this story about the women may be extending the discussion about the seventy-two earlier in Luke 10, a discussion that continues through the Samaritan story, and through the lesson given to a lawyer (10:25). If the overarching theme of the stories is about choosing Jesus and his message, then the mission of the seventy-two, the lesson to the lawyer of knowing and loving your neighbor, and also Jesus' response to Martha about Mary's choice being the better one are all connected with each other. They are all about knowing Jesus and what he stood for. The challenge to the recipients is to go outside the personal biases and *make the right choice*. What are those choices? Well, actually, there was only one. This one is the overarching theme of the three stories. The seventy-two were commissioned to go prepare the people to choose the Kingdom of God. The lawyer was asking about inheriting eternal life. Jesus responded by giving an example through the parable of the good Samaritan. Martha was directly instructed to choose the right thing to do—that is, to choose Jesus! Mary did.

## APPLICATION

The application of this history is quite simple. When Jesus came, people who responded to him as Lord broke the political and social conventions of their society. In the case of Mary, she broke convention for sure. Yet, the central theme of this story is not about being like Mary, but about the believer not being like Martha (as it did not clearly address Mary). All services were good in those days, but they were to be accompanied by the right attitude.

If we apply the passage to its historical background, Luke's portrait showed a radical gospel that valued breaking conventions for the sake of choosing Jesus. Ironically, this breaking of convention happened in the context of the conventions held by religious Jews. Unquestionably, the gospel is radically different from the world. Yet, Luke's exhortation went further to make the members of the church community examine some of their choices in creating certain conventions. In Mary's action, Jesus showed that even the conventions of faith communities demand further examination.

This passage also has nothing to do with a kind of passive Christianity that merely encourages believers to sit around to contemplate the meaning of life. Surely, there is a place for contemplation, but it does not come out of this passage. Neither does it come out of Mary's example.

## MISTAKES TO AVOID

The first mistake to avoid is dividing the story without noting its original context. We do not need to elaborate any longer on this point. The second mistake to avoid is ignoring the social context of the first century. The social background about first-century women seems very valuable in understanding this story. The third mistake to avoid is neglecting the wider context of Luke where women do play a serious role. The third mistake can only be rectified by reading more commentaries or studies on Luke or by reading Luke's narratives over and over again. Within a narrative, certain types of characters take on certain character traits that fit both the book context and the social background. The combination of these factors will shed light on the text.

## DISCUSSION QUESTIONS

- What is the problem with the popular interpretation of this story?
- Is Martha's service inherently bad? Why or why not?

*Luke 10:38–42—Submissive Mary Against Fussy Martha?*

- How is this story related to the surrounding context?
- What application can we draw from a context-based interpretation?

# 9

## Luke 11:1–13—
## The Lord's Prayer Only?

One day Jesus was praying in a certain place. When he finished, one of his disciples said to him, "Lord, teach us to pray, just as John taught his disciples."
He said to them, "When you pray, say:
"'Father, hallowed be your name, your kingdom come. Give us each day our daily bread. Forgive us our sins, for we also forgive everyone who sins against us. And lead us not into temptation.'"
Then Jesus said to them, "Suppose you have a friend, and you go to him at midnight and say, 'Friend, lend me three loaves of bread; a friend of mine on a journey has come to me, and I have no food to offer him.' And suppose the one inside answers, 'Don't bother me. The door is already locked, and my children and I are in bed. I can't get up and give you anything.' I tell you, even though he will not get up and give you the bread because of friendship, yet because of your shameless audacity he will surely get up and give you as much as you need.
"So I say to you: Ask and it will be given to you; seek and you will find; knock and the door will be opened to you. For everyone who asks receives; the one who seeks finds; and to the one who knocks, the door will be opened.
"Which of you fathers, if your son asks for a fish, will give him a snake instead? Or if he asks for an egg, will give him a scorpion? If you then, though you are evil, know how to give good gifts to your children, how much more will your Father in heaven give the Holy Spirit to those who ask him!"

*Luke 11:1–13—The Lord's Prayer Only?*

## THE POPULAR MEANING

People popularly see this as the Lord's Prayer and ignore everything else around it. Obviously, we do not want to change the designation of the "Lord's" prayer, as it is popularly construed. Yet, it is clear from this passage that we are better off calling it the "disciples' prayer taught by the Lord, but we shall see that it is so much more than a mere traditional prayer.

More popular meaning comes out of 11:9–10 by those who teach a prosperity gospel. They suggest that if we ask hard enough, God will grant the request. Worse yet, they may go further to suggest that as long as they get the result they're wishing for, God must be blessing them. Nothing is further from the truth, as we shall see below. The Bible is just not that simplistic. Reality is even more complicated.

Another popular way to understand this passage is to harmonize it with Matthew 6:9–13 and 7:7–12. I have already demonstrated above one case of harmonization that does not work. Harmonization does not work in general because any such effort yanks a passage from its original context by the original author and create some kind of new artificial formulation with new meanings.

These interpretive inaccuracies can only be cured by looking at the entire passage as a whole instead of seeing it as a collection of separate parts.

## WHERE DOES THE PASSAGE BEGIN?

The division of the passage is easy enough. Luke 11:1–13 is exactly the right division because this was a praying occasion, while 11:14 has a new occasion, an exorcism occasion. The occasion, and often location, is the best way to determine the division of a narrated event. Yet, let me remind my readers that we need to look at a passage as something that links together with its surrounding context, instead of cutting up its parts and mining them for our own agenda. In this case, the audience was Jesus' disciples.

## THE MEANING OF THE PASSAGE

The passage is divided into two basic parts with the phrase "he said to them" in 11:2, 5. Yet, these parts are related. I do not think I need to reiterate the basic meaning of the Lord's Prayer. The interested reader can consult many works on its meaning. The only thing I want to point out is the plural first person pronoun to indicate that prayer needs to respect what is beneficial for the entire community of believers and not just for individual interest. Jesus didn't use "me;" he used "us." The praying disciples were praying as a group. Of course, Jesus did not negate individual responsibility here. His emphasis however was on the corporate impact of individuals sinning against one another.

In 11:5–13, this second section can also divide into two parts. The division point should be "so I say to you" in 11:9 (to match 11:2, 5).[1] The first part narrates a parable about a needy person who makes a request. The vocabulary is driven by friendship. Thus, the foundation for asking something is friendship. Another lesson it teaches is "boldness" to ask. The boldness comes from friendship.

The part in 11:9–13 is trickier. It starts with a misunderstood passage about "ask, seek, knock" in 11:9. The intensifying tripartite command teaches persistence. Due to the fact that the section 11:9–10 belongs to 11:11–13, the latter further explains the former. The previous parable in 11:5–8 seems to point to persistence as being a key factor. Jesus wanted to make sure to address it. Is persistence enough? Will persistence change God's sovereign mind? Is the mere repetition of request the main factor to getting what "I" want for my prayer?

11:11–13 gives a very clear answer by a parable about the relationship between fathers and children. The parable came from a common human condition (11:11, 13). The parable is quite humorous if we think about the images. The fish looks like a snake and the egg looks like a scorpion. I often wonder if Jesus was telling a joke. The point is, only fish and eggs are good for the children. The Father knows best. In other words, the key issue is not persistence, even though persistence shows the sincerity of the person praying. The key issue is whether the request would be good for the children. Furthermore, we now go back to the entire context of the passage. Jesus had always been concerned about community benefit. These parables are individualistic simply because they help illustrate God's good will towards his children. If the Lord's Prayer is the foundation before these parables, we must read the parables as illustrations of the foundation. Community benefit and not self-interest is the foundation, based on Jesus' usage of the word "us" in the Lord's Prayer. If we make all the "us" into "me," the

---

1. 11:8 certainly has an "I say to you" saying as well, if we want to count it among such sayings, but its content shows that it is a explanation and not a final conclusion of the story. 11:9 also has a "you" in emphatic position to show a finality to the moral of the story.

prayer would actually sound quite different. Imagine saying, "Give me each day my daily bread." Surely, the corporate "us" with the singular "bread" has a different meaning than the individual "me" with the individual "bread." The example can multiply. The main key to answered prayer is not mere repetition but community benefit. Therefore, whenever we pray for our own need, we must also consider needs of the entire community.

## APPLICATION

Far from seeing the Lord's Prayer as something that changes the sovereign mind of God, Jesus was affirming the sovereign unchangeable will of God in this teaching. God knows what is best for his children. God's character is hardly on the mind of many popular preachers on prayer. Most of the time, it is about human effort and human agency in getting what "I" want in prayer. In Jesus' teaching, God's character was central to prayer. The very fact that believers come to God in prayer is an acknowledgement of divine sovereignty. God gives good gifts to believers who come before his throne of grace. It takes a certain amount of faith to believe that all good gifts come from above. Thus the human agency of faith in a loving God is what causes believers to come before his throne. When interpreters neglect divine character in prayer, they miss a large part of why people pray.

This issue of God's character though, is nuanced by the theme of friendship with God in the first parable of the friends. It is very important to appreciate these aspects before praying the Lord's Prayer. It is also important to keep in mind the benefits of the community when people pray because the Lord's Prayer was taught in community, evident by the usage of the word "us" rather than "me." By implication of this important prayer, self-centeredness is detrimental to healthy prayer life. Although prayer can be individual, it must keep in mind the corporate impact. When the disciples pray together, they are also mindful of each other's needs so that they can help each other. It is not enough to think about "me and myself" only when we pray. We need to ask God to illuminate our insights so that we can see the needs of others and serve them.

## MISTAKES TO AVOID

The harmonizing approach between Matthew and Luke is clearly the first mistake. Matthew 6 teaches the three acts of piety as "acts of righteousness"

(Matthew 6:1). Prayer is only one act of righteousness. Matthew's teaching merely uses prayer to talk about acts of righteousness. While the content is about prayer, it is used to discuss the greater issue of "acts of righteousness." The main thrust of Matthew is then about doing acts of righteousness, such as prayer, in front of God.

The main thrust of Luke is not talking about prayer as an act of righteousness so much as a condition under which answers to prayer can take place. Thus, Luke's focus is quite different from Matthew's. Although the differences may seem minor, they are enough to set our Bible study or preaching in different directions. Those who lead Bible studies or preach from these passages need to pay closer attention. Therefore, the harmonizing approach of similar accounts often (but not always) does more harm than good in terms of giving direction to our preaching or Bible study. It is a tool to be used discretely.

The second mistake to avoid is chopping up the passage apart from its context or its immediate audience (i.e., the disciples). If we keep the sections apart, they do not make sense and create huge theological problems. When we read the entire sermon together, every piece makes sense as part of a holistic message.

## DISCUSSION QUESTIONS

- What is wrong with the popular interpretations?
- What are the differences between the teachings about prayer in Matthew and Luke?
- What is the function of the fatherly gift in Luke 11:11–13?
- What is the main issue with prayer?

# 10

# Luke 15—
# Which Lost Son?

> "'My son,' the father said, 'you are always with me, and everything I have is yours. But we had to celebrate and be glad, because this brother of yours was dead and is alive again; he was lost and is found....'"

## THE POPULAR MEANING

THERE IS HARDLY A more well-loved story in the New Testament than the parable of the lost, or prodigal son. The story of the lost son talks of God's grace towards the younger son because he is the prodigal. At least, that is the common interpretation. One preacher says that God wanted to restore the family so bad that he would first allow the son to insult him and then run to him when the son returned. More common still is the tendency to see the parable as a separate parable from the previous two. We shall see in the discussion below that both common interpretations are incorrect.

There have been other interpretations of this passage that are equally unlikely but still quite popular among preachers. Some have even discussed the story as a lesson in parenting and that we ought to learn the parenting style of God the Father, symbolic in the father of the parable. Others see a radically different God (a "prodigal God") who does things contrary to human expectations. Others use the story as a model for sharing the gospel with the lost. Some of these interpretations may have a point, but all miss the precise meaning the entire sermon brings. I am convinced that without a more specific sense of Jesus' overall message in context, we cannot possibly apply the message correctly for today.

## WHERE DOES THE PASSAGE BEGIN?

The passage begins at 15:1. This is one chapter division that seems accurate to the narrative. The problem then, in this case, goes beyond chapter division. We must keep the lost son story within the entire narrative of Luke 15. Yet, reading the parable in Luke 15 does not represent the entire narrative that spans through 17:10. In such a case, our problem is not where the passage begins but where the entire sermon ends. The real question is, when did Jesus finally stop talking to the same audience, in the same location, and switch to a different audience and location? I shall talk about the parable in Luke 15 first before I go into Jesus' whole sermon. Even if we understand Luke 15 by itself, we will dispel a lot of misinterpretation of the prodigal son story popularized by typical Bible study and preaching. I suggest most do not even understand the content of Luke 15 by itself. Let us get to our task.

## THE MEANING OF THE PASSAGE

It is a mistake to single out the prodigal son story as a single parable as many scholars and popular preachers have done. I call Luke 15 the parable of the lost (and not only "lost son") because its three stories make up a singular parable marked by the singular noun "parable" (not plural "parables") in 15:3. All three stories contain the elements of lost and found, via repentance. Something as simple as the singular noun "parable" which describes not one but three stories needs to be taken very seriously. It is easy to see three parables because Jesus used "or" in 15.8 and then there was a cutoff at 15.11 with "Jesus continued." Nevertheless, the three stories must be read as one. The plot of the singular parable looks something like this:

| 15:3 | single parable to answer religious leaders |
| 15:4–7 | sheep: lost, found, rejoicing |
| 15:8–10 | coin: lost, found, rejoicing |
| 15:11–32 | son: lost, found, rejoicing (and not rejoicing) |

## Luke 15—Which Lost Son?

So, how can we interpret the three stories as a single parable? Since the verses 15:1–2 show the objection of the religious leaders, any meaning that does not answer that objection needs to be thrown out automatically.

For starters, the three stories in Luke 15 have the same plot structure, which answers the ridicule of the religious leaders. The story structure contains three elements: lost, found, and rejoicing. The one difference may be the usage of a Greek word for rejoicing for both the sheep and coin in 15:6 and 15:9 that is, however, different from the word for rejoicing for the son in 15:24. This is probably just a literary device to show the difference between things and humans.

Based on the discussion so far, those who focus on the third story are half correct. The difference does not stop at the word "rejoice" because the third story does not end with rejoicing but ends with the big brother being hesitant to enter the house to rejoice. Thus, the difference in the third story highlights the main point of the big brother due to an extra feature in 15:25–32 about the older brother. The extra feature about the older son, and not the return of the younger son (as popularly understood), is the climax of the story.

Jesus broke the story patterns of the previous stories to highlight the older son. If the story plot of lost, found, and rejoice still holds true, the formerly lost young son remains quite important, but now that the older son comes into play, the shift of focus shows that the story really is a contrast between the younger and older son with the former being firmly inside the father's house and the latter being hesitant to enter because his younger brother is there. Unlike the tax gatherers and sinners who were now found, the big brother (typifying the religious leaders) is ironically in danger of being lost.

The negative character, the big brother, like many of Luke's negative characters is not entirely devoid of goodness. While the younger son squandered the father's inheritance, the older son was serving the father. Yet, there was something slightly different in the way the older son described his younger brother than Jesus' description. While Jesus the narrator talked about the younger brother's lifestyle as being a kind of "wild living," the older son focused on the specific detail of consorting with prostitutes in 15:30. We cannot be sure whether the older son was telling the entire truth or was making things up to blacken his brother's name. No matter what, the narrative illustrates the attitude that resembles the Pharisees' who objected to the company Jesus kept. The older son was much like those Pharisees, as he was still lost. The artful storytelling of Jesus sent a clear message: the lost son was the older son!

Now that we have determined the lost son was really the older son, we need to look at the wider narrative context in order to appreciate what Jesus was saying. While the parable of the lost addressed the Pharisees, the next story Jesus told (the parable of the shrewd manager) also dealt with the Pharisees. Even though in both, the disciples learned a lesson, the Pharisees were always within earshot of Jesus' teaching. One aspect of the older son's mistake was his focus on the squandered material wealth of his younger brother instead of focusing on his relationship with his younger brother. The repeated relational vocabulary such as "father," "brother," or "son" in 15:27, 30, 31–32, shows the importance of relationships. The older brother merely called his brother "this younger son of *yours*" (to his father) in 15:30 in his complaint about property. Luke 15 is the perfect preface to 16:1–15. There is so much more I can say, but I shall talk about it in my study below on Luke 16. For now, the wider narrative context shows Jesus to continue his condemnation of the Pharisees.

## APPLICATION

"Pharisee" has been used as a derisive metaphor for all kinds of people we dislike, but we must be sure that the Pharisees in Jesus' time were very righteous and orthodox people. We must note that Jesus' condemnation here of the Pharisees was very specific. They were at fault for two specific offenses. First, they received condemnation for their role in rejecting those like the "younger brothers." Second, they received condemnation for their love of money. We shall see shortly, in Luke 16, that their love of money coheres well with the entire narrative as well as the story of the lost son. For now, Jesus' condemnation was against anyone who cared more about appearing holy than about full acceptance of repentant sinners. Such a person is lost, according to the parable.

Although many Christians pay lip service to "salvation by grace alone," they practice something entirely different. Grace-filled living means forgiving and pitying the weaker and immoral trespasser. When we examine how some ministries are run, we can clearly see the limitation of Christian grace. I recall one instance in a church where parents allowed their children to go on short-term missions, but were totally against outreach to the local poor. Why? It was because they were afraid that such lost sinners might come to

*Luke 15—Which Lost Son?*

church and contaminate their children, instead of seeing the transforming power of the Christian faith and community for such sinners that they, too, can sit at God's banquet. This is a double standard that goes against Jesus' ethics. If people really believe in God's power, they must also act upon that conviction.

## MISTAKES TO AVOID

The exegetical mistakes to avoid are several. The first is the failure to take seriously where the narrative begins. Along with this mistake is the necessary awareness of where the narrative ends. We shall explore Luke 16 below to make sure we fully appreciate the entire narrative running from 15:1—17:10. Second, the mistake of overlooking the singular "parable" in 15:3 is almost elementary, but so many books and "experts" continue to make this simple mistake. If we just take the time to read the text, we shall reap benefits. In this case, our awareness brings us a new highlight Jesus meant for his audience to hear. So, watch out for singular versus plural nouns. Even for my readers who do not read Greek, most English translations provide footnotes to indicate whether nouns are singular or plural.

When dealing with any parable, we should treat it neither as a sermon only nor as a narrative only. If there is a narrative element in it, we must then look closely at the narrative. One issue we need to note in looking at a narrative, in addition to being aware of the plot structure and the origin of the story, is the character development. Characters in narratives can have typological functions. We should be aware of "how" the author characterizes a character as much as "who" the character is. The "who" only identifies the character while the "how" shows how the character functions within the narrative.

## DISCUSSION QUESTIONS

- What is wrong with the popular interpretation?
- What is the key to understanding a story with multiple parts?
- How does the story address the Pharisees' concern?
- What kind of similar problems do we see in our churches today?

# 11

## Luke 16:1–15— Dishonesty and Divorce?

Jesus told his disciples: "There was a rich man whose manager was accused of wasting his possessions. So he called him in and asked him, 'What is this I hear about you? Give an account of your management, because you cannot be manager any longer.'

"The manager said to himself, 'What shall I do now? My master is taking away my job. I'm not strong enough to dig, and I'm ashamed to beg—I know what I'll do so that, when I lose my job here, people will welcome me into their houses.'

"So he called in each one of his master's debtors. He asked the first, 'How much do you owe my master?'

"'Nine hundred gallons of olive oil,' he replied.

"The manager told him, 'Take your bill, sit down quickly, and make it four hundred and fifty.'

"Then he asked the second, 'And how much do you owe?'

"'A thousand bushels of wheat,' he replied.

"He told him, 'Take your bill and make it eight hundred.'

"The master commended the dishonest manager because he had acted shrewdly. For the people of this world are more shrewd in dealing with their own kind than are the people of the light. I tell you, use worldly wealth to gain friends for yourselves, so that when it is gone, you will be welcomed into eternal dwellings....''

*Luke 16:1–15—Dishonesty and Divorce?*

## THE POPULAR MEANING

THERE IS HARDLY A popular meaning, only muddled musings, for Luke 16:1–15, as it presents huge difficulties for interpreters. Instead, too many meanings come out of it. The New International Version's translation of this passage divides (wrongly) at 16:15 and 16:18, giving the passage some meanings unconnected to the overall message. A popular meaning for 16:16–18 is that the section is about divorce. The section 16:19–31 normally is taken to talk about Jesus' condemnation of the rich. Such a fragmented way to interpret Jesus' sermon seems to see Jesus as some kind of incoherent creator of proverbial expressions, commenting about life in general. Jesus then becomes some kind of religious sage who says everything and anything about all topics of his day and ours, without any context of any kind. As we shall see below, Jesus' sermon here is quite logically a progression from 15:1—17:10. Much of the popular meaning is lacking. My reader will have to bear with me as we study Luke 16, because it is a little bit involved and challenging. The end result, however, will be more fruitful than imagined.

## WHERE DOES THE PASSAGE BEGIN?

This question does not need elaboration because of the previous discussion on Luke 15. As we have said before, the entire event that led up to this parable comes from Luke 15, which does not end until 17:10. The reason we can expand the parable to 17:10 is because 17:11 describes Jesus moving to a different place. In other words, the way we understand the overall story still depends on how certain events transpire in a certain setting, before the narrative moves on to another setting. Therefore, the historical events and circumstance stimulate the telling of parables. This strategy of reading proves more challenging for the interpreter, but the rewards are great because we will look at the entire sermon from Jesus as a whole, and not some random fragments.

## THE MEANING OF THE PASSAGE

Like any narrative, a problem was the occasion for this story. In 16:1, Jesus told the story to the disciples about a wasteful manager. It is probably wise to see a slight separation from 15:32 because Luke inserted 16:1 as a break. Thus, Luke 15 contains one parable with three stories. In a Roman household, the manager's job was to make sure resources were distributed evenly and invested wisely. This manager apparently mismanaged resources. His problem progressed from bad to worse when he was fired in 16:2. He responded by coming up with a solution in 16:3–7, cutting the debts of those who owed his master (most likely behind his master's back) until it was too late for the master to undo the damage. Instead of getting a scolding from an angry master, the manager was surprisingly praised in 16:8. The manager's problem was not the lack of intelligence, because he surely took care of his own needs very well.

This story by itself makes little sense because the manager still did not get back all his master's investment. At best, he had helped the master cut losses that the debtors were not going to pay anyway. At worst, he had lost more of his master's money. Yet, his master praised him. The story has a surprise ending that requires further explanation. Jesus called the manager's values as coming from "people of this world/age" in 16:8b. To what values was Jesus referring? Jesus was certainly not advocating deception. Jesus used the surprising ending to shock his audience into paying close attention to the main point. Jesus gave the explanation in 16:8–13.

Before Jesus' explanation, we must first appreciate the way Jesus told the parable. In 16:3, we hear the manager talking to himself, presumably in his mind. This hidden conversation shows the motive behind the manager's action. This hidden conversation then becomes a large part of what Jesus based his explanation on because it does not merely deal with the manager's action, but his mentality. Based on Jesus' artistic framing of the parable, the manager's mentality rather than his action should be the focus of the story. Quite often, commentators question his action rather than his inner voice, while Jesus seems to focus on the inner voice of the manager in 16:3.

Jesus started commenting on this parable starting at 16:8b–9. The shift in tone is especially important in 16:9 because the parable now is applied to "you;" Jesus was no longer talking about the parable in third person but was addressing the disciples in plural second person pronoun. The discussion centered on the idea of the shrewdness, in 16:9, of using financial means not so much to build up personal portfolio, but to gain friends. Jesus discussed three issues on shrewdness while departing from the previous story. First, he talked about trustworthiness in 16:10–12, indirectly condemning the manager's untrustworthy stewardship. At the same time, Jesus' comment shows that being a good steward of someone else's stuff can result in being rewarded "your own property." Second, Jesus talked about serving the right master in 16:13 because the discussion is already transitioning away from the parable to the discussion about the master. This further highlights the manager's unfaithfulness to his master, but at the same time advocates serving Jesus, the right master. Third, the above two issues pointed to Jesus' affirmation of the importance of relationship over money. Good stewardship comes from prioritizing relationship over money, thus reaping greater reward from God. Thus, the manager is also used to reflect the positive usage of money to gain relationships.

In light of relationship discussions, Jesus further affirmed that the most important relationship was not merely with people but ultimately with God (16:13). Yet, relationships with people and devotion to God appear to be linked because both have a monetary aspect to them (16:13). There is no confusion as to which part of the parable was the main point, and which parts were subsidiary points. The main point remained with the inner voice of the manager in 16:3, while the rest of the manager's dishonest deeds were subsidiary points to illustrate how he fulfilled his main goal. Jesus was not suggesting the manager's method was right. In fact, he condemned any unfaithful stewardship in 16:10–12. Rather, he approved of his relationship-centered usage of his money, power, and position.

The parable resulted in Pharisees sneering at Jesus in 16:14, which led Jesus to condemn their love of money. What then should be in the human heart, based on the entire sermon? The story seems to show that the human heart should focus on relationship, first with God as his Lord and second on others whose relationships would prove valuable for eternity. To Luke, the only thing that lasts will be human relationships built on obeying God, and not love of money. The parable of the shrewd manager has meaning in the wider context, at least within its immediate surroundings. The parable touches on Luke's view of wealth. Since the context concerns the entire narrative, our task of interpretation is not done yet.

We have now come to the thorny part of our interpretive journey. Many commentators find 16:16–18 to be problematic. Some may see it as an awkward insertion. One translation adds a section heading that suggests Jesus was giving an additional teaching that was totally unrelated to the previous parable. In light of the confusion, I conclude that interpreters are not trying hard enough to read 16:16–18 in context. Let me suggest a way forward which must shed light on the parable of the shrewd manager and the Lazarus story in a later discussion. But let me first deal with the Lazarus story in light of the shrewd manager story, because after all, the Lazarus story seems more straightforward.

The parable of the rich man and Lazarus in 16:19–31 appears to be a stark contrast between the rich and the poor. Like some kind of muddled fable, it contains details that are esoteric at best, resulting in vast range of interpretations beyond the space of this chapter. In order to find the right focus, we have to first determine who the main characters are.

I suggest the rich man and Abraham as the main characters simply because these two are the only ones talking while Lazarus stays silent. Lazarus is a foil for this conversation between the two other characters. The story seems to show how the rich man ends up where he is by showing highlights of his life before he died. His life before death leads to the life after. The focus of the Lazarus story is on the rich man and what he has done to deserve *his* eternal abode. It is incorrect to focus on poor Lazarus because he does not play a major part. Therefore, we may never find the answer as to why Lazarus ended up in the good eternal abode. Neither Jesus nor Luke indicated any reason. It is therefore, a mistake to focus on Lazarus's salvation.

When reading correctly in light of the context of the previous parable, it is not hard to isolate a particular thread having to do with the rich man's treatment of Lazarus in 16:19–21, because so much of this description of his earthly life is focused on his treatment of Lazarus and not on the "character" or "virtues" of poor Lazarus. The "relationship" thread continues. Lazarus appears to have depended on the rich man's sponsorship, but was not able to get much of anything. The fortunes of the two men were reversed when each died. The rich man, in Hades, requested that Lazarus be sent to warn his family. Abraham's answer was that if they did not listen to Moses and the Prophets, they would certainly not listen to a resurrected man. The reference to Moses and the Prophets is another way of pointing to 16:16. It was all part of a sermon. What then did Jesus mean when he referred to Moses and the Prophets? This can only be answered by looking at 16:16–18.

Jesus' sermon had not ended yet, as he continued teaching in 16:16–17. The section 16:16–18 is indeed a puzzling section. But in the end it is simpler than it appears. The description of 16:16b is about the urgency of the kingdom. Naturally, Jesus was referring to his own preaching because he was the only one preaching in this passage. Since the kingdom's call was so urgent, the proper response was to want to get in, instead of "sneering" at Jesus like the Pharisees (16:14). The proper response, specifically, was to abandon the money the Pharisees loved and begin building relationships

## Luke 16:1–15—Dishonesty and Divorce?

with sinners and outsiders. This relational aspect was definitely part of the kingdom preaching in this text. The discussion of the Law and the Prophets should link back to the message of Jesus against the Pharisees who loved money. Their sneering was a response against the parable of the shrewd manager. These seemingly separate elements then are related in the overall scheme of the storyline. In other words, Jesus' teachings about the Law and Prophets were about the just use of resources to build just relationships. The seriousness of this aspect was stated in 16:17.

The puzzling discussion about divorce in 16:18 is, in reality, not about divorce at all. Why did Jesus talk about divorce when marriage is not even a topic within the entire narrative? The answer should appear simple by now. Divorce shows a broken relationship that has originally been covenanted within the Old Testament law. In the Old Testament, marriage is the first relationship God created. Thus, the teaching on divorce serves to illustrate how serious God takes relationship. God never sees the marital covenant as nullified. Otherwise how would the person who remarries commit adultery? In terms of human laws, adultery only happens when a partner is having sexual relationship with another while being married. In terms of God's law, that relationship should have never been broken, thus causing remarriage to be an adulterous act, even if the divorcee no longer has sexual relationship with the former spouse. The moral lesson is that God takes relationship seriously, which leads nicely to the next section on forgiveness, which is also about relationship.

The narrative goes further as Jesus taught about forgiveness and faith in 17:1–10 in this plot development. In 17:1–10, the discussion still centers on relationship. Jesus encouraged the apostles to watch out so that they did not cause the little ones to stumble. Then, the brother who sinned and repented seven times needed to be forgiven. This amplifies the degree of forgiveness far beyond the grave sin of the prodigal son in chapter 15. Curiously, the apostles asked the Lord to increase their faith in 17:5. "Increase our faith," they said. Jesus only replied that it took so little faith to forgive that barely any faith would be needed at all. To Jesus however, faith was not the problem. By using hyperbole, Jesus was ready to dismiss the disciples' notion of needing faith to forgive.

What do the little ones and the repentant brother have in common? They both deal with relationships of various kinds, from a weak person to a repeated offender. Jesus went on to talk about a parable where a servant needed to do his duty in 17:7–10. Good relationship is not about faith, as the apostles presumed, but is about duties, as the parable seems to illustrate. Jesus turned their attention from faith to duty starting at 17:17. What duties was Jesus talking about? The duties include everything in 16:1—17:10, all summarized in one phrase: relationships as duty. If the disciple realizes that relationship is above all things, then he would not have a problem investing in relationships, or forgiving the sinner, or any other duty. Jesus wanted to teach one thing through the entire sermon: value relationships above all things. What kind of relationships? Based on the wide narrative spanning 15:1—17:10, the community should build relationships with tax gatherers, sinners, and the poor (e.g., the likes of Lazarus).

We have now come to the key to understanding both the shrewd manager and Lazarus stories. Instead of focusing on the content of 16:16–18, we need to ask what this section is doing in the wider sermon and narrative. Instead of assuming Jesus was a random speaker of wise sayings, we can ask what Jesus was doing in putting this section at this junction between two parables. The section of 16:16–18 is a bridge from the shrewd manager story to the parable of Lazarus, in the remaining part of the chapter. It is a sermon transition that concludes the shrewd manager's story but at the same time introduces the Lazarus story.

In terms of events and topics that led up to Jesus' dialogue with the Pharisees, Jesus was dealing with human relations: relationships between the father, older son, and younger, as an analogical topic to talk about something else: lasting relationship and commitment to one person. The discussion about the eternal duration of the Law in 16:17 is also not merely a general statement, but it introduces the topic of divorce. Jesus' discussion of divorce here was implicated in the Old Testament. In other words, when Jesus talked about duration of the Law, he included the very important and relevant example of marital relationship. In turn, the marital covenant illustrates the importance of relationship to God. Commitment to relationship should not be easily discarded. Furthermore, the commitment issue has been discussed just now in 16:13 between the disciples and God. Thus, the divorce topic points back to the relationship discussion of the shrewd manager, and at the same time points to commitment the disciples should have.

Like the marriage relationship and covenant, once the disciples started their membership in the kingdom, as in 16:16, they were committed to God wholeheartedly. If our assessment is correct, from 16:16–18 Jesus was referring to prioritizing godly relationship over money in the Lazarus story by referring to "Moses and the Prophets" again (cf. 16:16–17; 16:29). In other

*Luke 16:1-15—Dishonesty and Divorce?*

words, the kingdom citizen would not love money but would prioritize relationships.

Let me now summarize the meaning included in 15:1—17:10. The parable of the lost (sheep/coin/son) shows negatively a bad relationship in the kingdom, exemplified by the older son and the Pharisees. The parable of the manager shows positively that relationships are indeed important. The parable of the rich man and Lazarus condemns the bad relationships. The final conclusion talks about the duty to make relationships with the sinners and tax collectors of Luke 15, and with the little ones of Luke 17.

In contrast to the kind of exclusionary religious leadership in the text, Jesus' parables have an inclusive and outreaching application. To Jesus, the only good money was the money the disciple gave away (or invested) towards kingdom relationships. The parable of the lost shows the importance of building relationship with the fringe group (e.g., sinners and tax collectors). The shrewd manager shows the importance of relationship over money, aptly illustrated in the Lazarus story. The section 17:1-10 shows the importance of duty to the Lord, specifically to forgive. What is duty in light of the entire 15:1—17:10? Isn't it to forgive, befriend, and build relationships with those on the outside of the normal religious sphere (e.g., sinners, tax collectors, Lazarus)? Therefore, I have demonstrated the importance of keeping the entire story together and letting each part give meaning to each other. Logically, 17:1-10 wraps up the entire discussion very well. Jesus ended 15:1—17:10 on the issue with which he began: relationships.

## APPLICATION

The macroscopic reading of 16:1-15 proves decisively where the limit of interpretation is. The story started with the narrator peering into the mind of the shrewd manager. Actually, the story fits in the parable before where the Pharisees got condemned for their attitude towards sinners. This story condemned also their love of money. Both harm kingdom relationships. The rest of 16:1—17:10 focuses more or less on different aspects of relationships, each one more precisely defining what Jesus meant by relationship.

In summary, this self-contained story clearly sets qualifiers on the message of the parable. First, the message was not for the disciples to imitate the ethics of the manager. Jesus already denounced dishonesty. Second, the message was about the proper usage of personal resources. Third, the message linked the Lordship of God with human relationships. In other words, the truly loyal kingdom citizen would honor others with his wealth in order to express his honor of God. The wealth the citizen handles reflects the recognition of Jesus' lordship. Luke was challenging his audience to give wealth to those in need for the kingdom. Thus, contrary to appearance, the Lordship of God, or of Christ, is not an abstract theological concept with no application.

In today's world, we can make a general observation that the more people love material wealth, the less they love God and other humans. Material goods can also cause unnecessary conflicts when someone trespasses on our interest. Most likely, the trouble is the pressure of materialistic living. In many big cities where the standard of living is expensive, people are also generally ruder. Rather than sharing, people need to horde to survive in such places. The church is especially important in such situations. It needs to exemplify generosity. Individual giving is not enough because there are also many poor folks in church. Giving must be corporate in order to build sound relationships.

## MISTAKES TO AVOID

Of all the examples, the discussion about the lost son demands a holistic treatment of a narrative. The mistake many make in reading any of the parables is the lack of appreciation for Jesus' message. Jesus' message is so much broader than our popular understanding.

Like many parables, the sermon itself has a storyline, a kind of ongoing narrative element. Not only is there a narrative element, but the sermon ties together the narratives it contains into a unified whole with one major principle in mind. As a sermon, every part fits like a jigsaw puzzle. If this unity principle is violated, then the meaning may be lost. The wider context should include the events that surround the telling of the parables. In other words, the interpreter needs to ask the question of the text, "How did this parable come about?" The interpreter must keep within his sight the beginning and the ending of the event that contains the telling of the parable. Without such macroscopic view, it is impossible to understand the parable.

Another mistake is to avoid is thinking that the difficult parts of a narrative or sermon (e.g., 16:16–18) are merely some random sayings of Jesus. This mistake is quite common because it focuses on content only and neglects the rhetorical purpose of the hard saying. Thus, any interpretation that does not explain where each part fits the narrative would be partial, at best, and inaccurate, at worst.

## DISCUSSION QUESTIONS

- Why is the story of the unjust steward so puzzling?
- Did Jesus teach his followers to be dishonest? Why or why not?
- What is worth learning from the unjust steward?
- How is the divorce passage linked with the surrounding discussion?
- What can the rich man and Lazarus story teach, and not teach?
- Who are the main characters (and why) in the rich man and Lazarus story?
- What is the main point related to the entire 15:1—17:10 passage?
- How are the lessons relevant to churches today?

# 12

## Luke 21:1–4—
## A Lesson on Sacrificial Giving?

As Jesus looked up, he saw the rich putting their gifts into the temple treasury. He also saw a poor widow put in two very small copper coins. "Truly I tell you," he said, "this poor widow has put in more than all the others. All these people gave their gifts out of their wealth; but she out of her poverty put in all she had to live on."

### THE POPULAR MEANING

This story has to rank among the all-time most misunderstood portions of Jesus' teaching. The general understanding views the widow's giving as a moral example. "Widow's mites" has become the synonym of sacrificial giving in our churches. This is almost the only popular view of the widow. Most of such understandings are based on sentimental preaching rather than strict interpretation. After all, if it preaches well, what can go wrong? Apparently, a lot can actually go wrong! Just because something touches the audience's emotion from the pulpit doesn't make it an accurate interpretation. Just because there has been a long tradition of exegesis, doesn't mean that the interpretation cannot be improved upon or even corrected. We shall see that Jesus' teaching is actually the opposite.

Strictly speaking, this story ought to belong to a strictly narrative discussion, but we shall see, based on the division of the passage, the narrative

*Luke 21:1-4—A Lesson on Sacrificial Giving?*

should be seen as a transition between (and therefore connected to) sermons. The problem with most interpreters comes from seeing the story as purely narrative without considering what Jesus really was teaching. We shall see that the surrounding sermons should define the meaning of this narrative. Luke could have put this story before or after the sermons, but why did he put it between two major sermons? The answer will be illuminating to the meaning of the story.

## WHERE DOES THE PASSAGE BEGIN?

The passage does not begin in 21:1. Rather, it begins in 20:1 with "one day." Luke thus portrayed the rest as one single event within a single day until 21:36. The widow story is stuck at the tail end of the entire narrative. The story also transitions straight into Jesus' sermon about Jerusalem and the signs of the Son of Man's coming. These are indispensible points in understanding the passage.

## THE MEANING OF THE PASSAGE

Many popular sentimental preachers miss the obvious principle that should have been learned and applied in a basic course on interpretation in seminary: context. The immediate context of Luke 20–21 shows the obvious point Jesus was making. The widow was in such a sorry state because of the unnecessary social oppression that had fallen upon them in 20:46–47. We must note especially the change from "widow" in 20:47 to "poor widow" in 21:2. In the Greek, the word "poor" means "destitute."

In our story, Jesus observed in 21:1 an unpleasant contrast between the rich and the poor at the temple treasury. Based on the context of 20:47, Luke emphasized her process of being poor having something to do with the unjust system she unfortunately served. She ended up being this way because someone had oppressed her. The widow only had little to give simply because she was one of those who had lost a fortune to the hypocrites in 20:45–47. This discussion of justice confirms the woes against the Pharisees and law teachers in 11:37–54. The widow's coins became the perfect example of injustice. When Jesus saw her, he pointed to her as an example of that oppression first and foremost in light of 20:46–47. Luke probably would call this story a lament over the state of injustice in Israel. In other words, the society that brought her down deserved condemnation. Thus,

73

she represented all those who lived piously but anonymously because of social oppression.

Based on the above discussion, the best place Jesus demonstrated the injustice of Israel comes in the form of the widow's coins in 21:1–4. In pointing her out, Jesus was condemning her oppressor. Jesus did not commend her giving at all. He was merely pointing out the contrast between the rich and the poor. In popular interpretation, the giving dimension of 21:1–4 is often noted. It is however not enough to read the story as a giving story because Jesus did not explicitly talk about her giving being exemplary, just being greater in percentage than most.

The less noted but very important meaning of this story should connect with the other widow story in 18:1–8. While the parable of 18:1–8 no doubt demonstrates God's justice towards the oppressed, the oppressed widow theme also fits 20:47. If we remove the moral example interpretation for a minute, Jesus might even be condemning the temple-synagogue as the unjust institution that deserved nothing from the already poor widow. She had apparently given wrongly to an undeserving religious system. Luke did not finish his stories but allowed them to linger on to another similar theme to reiterate a point: Israel was full of injustices.

Now that we have entertained the possibility of an alternate interpretation, let us verify through surrounding contexts whether our interpretation is verifiable. The widow story, if it is about giving sacrificially, does not fit what came before; this is for sure. The application towards giving also does not fit what comes after in 21:5–36. The condemnation against the temple is the topic of 21:5–36. It seems quite a contradiction to encourage people to give sacrificially to a dying institution because Jesus had just predicted the demise of the temple. If anything, those who were involved with Israel's religion were more concerned about lining their own pockets. On the outside, they pretended that they cared about whether people gave to Caesar or God (cf. 20:19–26), but were in fact robbing God. In such a case, the only way the widow story will make sense is to see it as part of the explanation as to why the temple would get destroyed: it ripped off widows like this poor woman. The story then becomes a condemnation of any society or religious institution that takes advantage of the poor. It calls for reform of such a society to give up the self-interest of the elite so that the people can live better.

*Luke 21:1–4—A Lesson on Sacrificial Giving?*

## APPLICATION

The common interpretation of seeing this as a giving passage goes directly against the thrust of this story. With the choruses of condemnation surrounding the widow story, Jesus was condemning on the one hand, and was teaching about giving cautiously on the other, but not in the way we expect. If the modern Christian should give, he is to think hard before parting with his money for unworthy causes. This is not always the case with Christianity in recent years. Many generous offerings go to waste, to institutions and organizations that are unworthy of the gospel cause. But people give only because someone shouts, "We're reaching this many unreached people."

Another way to look at this passage is to hear the importance of integrity when funding religious activities. Those who prey on the needy would receive a harsh condemnation by Jesus. This is especially true in recent blossoming of Christian organizations, all clamoring for the church's resources. Many such organizations have hidden agendas and questionable methods. Although some claim to be doing evangelistic ministry, evangelism has become the excuse for all kinds of dubious practices and theologies. I personally experienced the impact of such organizations when I was teaching in Hong Kong, where some claim to have found Noah's Ark with no academic and ecclesiastical due process. Yet, at the same time, such organizations are raising millions yearly from new and naïve donors. Jesus' teaching actually encouraged his followers to exercise generosity *and* extreme caution and critical discernment. Money should be donated to the right causes, only after identifying the essential qualities of the kingdom stated by Jesus.

## MISTAKES TO AVOID

The mistake to avoid is to trust chapter divisions or topical divisions supplied by English translations of the Bible. We must also resist the moralizing tendency of pietistic applications before we do detailed reading of any text. The commendation of widow's offering as an ethical example does nothing to illuminate the condemnation following 21:5. The lack of coherence makes the widow's ethical example suspect. It is because it is not an ethical story but a condemnatory story. Overall, this story should be treated as part of a sermon prior or subsequent to it. It is not the main point of Jesus' teaching.

## DISCUSSION QUESTIONS

- What is wrong with the popular understanding of the widow's mites?
- How does the context address her plight?
- What are some of the themes that concerned Jesus in the surrounding context?
- How does reading the entire Gospel according to Luke help understand this story?
- How does this story become ethically applicable in today's world?

# 13

# John 10:1–21—
# A Lesson about Shepherding?

"Very truly I tell you Pharisees, anyone who does not enter the sheep pen by the gate, but climbs in by some other way, is a thief and a robber. The one who enters by the gate is the shepherd of the sheep...."

Therefore Jesus said again, "Very truly I tell you, I am the gate for the sheep. All who have come before me are thieves and robbers, but the sheep have not listened to them. I am the gate; whoever enters through me will be saved. They will come in and go out, and find pasture. The thief comes only to steal and kill and destroy; I have come that they may have life, and have it to the full...."

## THE POPULAR MEANING

JOHN 10 HAS BEEN viewed as the model passage for shepherding sheep. Countless sermons are preached on characteristics of a good shepherd versus a bad one. Some may use this sermon as an ethical example for pastors. Is this the true intent behind the composition of the passage? The discussion will show that the passage contains material about a shepherd, but it is not really about "how to be a shepherd." In this study, we will see the importance of considering a narrative plot when a sermon is related to the narrative.

## WHERE DOES THE PASSAGE BEGIN?

The question of where John 10 begins should intrigue every single interpreter because it is crucial in giving meaning and determining the genre of John 10. The section contains the teaching and the sign in 10:1–42, but it also continues the conversation started by Jesus in 9:41. This chapter is Jesus' answer to the conflict brought forth by the healing of the blind man. It has more than a superficial link with the story of the blind man as the debate about this man rages on in 10:21. This place is a typical example of the need to ignore chapter divisions artificially constructed by later Bible translators and interpreters. More importantly, like Matthew, John's narrative has a very intentional structure with repeated themes that can illuminate any given sermon. So, we must consider the broad book context as well.

## THE MEANING OF THE PASSAGE

Some observations are in order before we can get the meaning of this passage. Based on a plain reading of the narrative, there is no indicator of a clear break with 9:41. It is therefore very important to understand the plot of the blind man story.

One Sabbath (9:14), Jesus went along and saw a man born blind (9:1). His disciples questioned whether this man or his parents sinned to cause blindness (9:2). Jesus said that neither was at fault, but that the subsequent miracle was to display God's work (9:3). Then the story should answer this question, "What work of God is being displayed through the miracle?" Jesus healed the man through an unconventional method causing a series of events to follow.

First, a debate broke out among the bystanders (9:8–12), causing the man to recount how he was healed (9:11). Second, the Pharisees questioned the man and his parents because the healing was on a Sabbath (9:13–23). In the questioning, the looming danger of being kicked out of the community was present (9:22). Third, the Pharisees continued to question and debate vigorously with the man (9:24–33), leading to the man's expulsion from the synagogue (9:34). Jesus found the man and accepted him into his fold (9:35–38). How then do we know that the Pharisees were wrong and Jesus was right, other than our common knowledge from our Bible study? Without a doubt, the miracle validated Jesus earlier answer to his disciples about why the miracle was taking place (cf. 9:2–3). Thus, the disciples' question of whether this man or his parents were responsible for his blindness due to their sin was an inappropriate question. Jesus' miracle proved his own correctness. Yet, the Pharisees came to the same conclusion as the disciples (9:34; cf. 9:2).

It is important to summarize what work of God (9:3) had been displayed at this juncture. First, the miracle showed Jesus' correctness against the Pharisees. Second, the miracle showed Jesus to be the Son of God. The work of God not only showed Jesus' authority, but also condemned some of the institutional religious practices of Jesus' opponents. The work of God shows what God was "against" as much as what God was for. With an understanding of what led to the shepherd sermon, we are now ready to interpret the sermon.

When reading the entire sermon, there is a great need to read in wider context of John's narrative because it belongs to John's discussion of the temple as a prevailing theme in the entire Gospel. The problem of religion is very clear if we relate the shepherd sermon back to chapter 9. The false shepherd in 10:1b, 5–6 is shown to be robber and thief. Here, instead of drawing the man into Israel's sheepfold as they conceived it, the Jews threw the man out in 9:34, an action befitting robbers.

John used the story to create a series of contrasts between Jesus and the religious leaders. The religious leaders who came before Jesus were robbers, while Jesus was the good shepherd. The robbers rejected the blind man while Jesus accepted him. Within the narrative structure of John 9–10, those came before Jesus were the religious leaders. As it turns out, Jesus became absent after he healed the man while the man struggled with the robbers / spiritual leaders within the church. Jesus only came and found the blind man later.

The pronouncement on thieves and robbers in the shepherd discourse is directed at the progression of the blind man's story. Thus, the shepherd sermon both describes the situation of the blind man but at the same time attacks the religious institution of Jesus' audience. Jesus did not mean to attack the Old Testament prophets. Instead, he was attacking the religious leaders who persecuted the blind man. Jesus was following the order of how these events transpired in the narrative.

In this sermon, Jesus gave two metaphors of shepherd and door to describe himself as the solution to the present problem. Both metaphors must be related to the temple since both festivals were not only located at the temple, they were also related theologically to the temple. Jesus provided the solution to meeting God by doing the job of a good shepherd in 10:11–13. The shepherd metaphor was the dominant metaphor, involving sacrifice in 10:11–18. This sermon foreshadows the Passion. How is the shepherd related to the temple? He not only was the way to God, but also led the way to God because after his death, he literally went back to God the Father (20:17). Thus, all these pronouncements had prophetic value.

Jesus also talked about a prophecy for the future mission of the church in 10:14–18, where he would elect "other sheep." Other prophetic elements include the announcement of Jesus' authority to take up his life again, signifying God's vindication of Jesus' innocence at the resurrection. The same word "authority" is also used in 19:11, where Jesus talks of God's control over Pilate. His power would further demonstrate itself when Lazarus was called out at the grave in the next chapter. Lazarus' resurrection is worth discussing later.

The second metaphor Jesus used is the "door" in 10:7–10. This architectural analogy also fits the temple imagery. The shepherd illustrates authority, leadership (10:4), and care (10:3). The door illustrates protection (10:9a), freedom (10:9b), and nurture (10.9b). In addition, if we consider the temple problem, we must consider the door as part of the building leading to the Father. Interestingly, the door that led to God would be the original function of the temple. Jesus had transformed the temple tradition into a living door embodied in his person. This too will become significant as we discuss the wider context of John.

With these combined metaphors and the subsequent pronouncements, we can begin to formulate what Jesus says about himself. First, we must notice the exclusivity of Jesus' claim in direct rivalry with the temple's or the synagogue's claim over those under its control (10:25–38). Jesus showed that his followers are exclusively elected in 10:26 with the contrast of two kinds of people. Those who were elected to be his sheep belonged to the first kind. Those who were not belong to the second kind. The main difference was that the first group has faith. Jesus also expressed an exclusive attribute that distinguishes him from any other human. In 10:30, he claims "I and the Father are one." Even though Jesus and the Father were not the same "person," they had the same attributes. Which attribute does Jesus have in mind? The divinity of Israel's "shepherd" YHWH became Jesus' attribute. In other words, YHWH was Israel's shepherd but now Jesus took on the role.

## John 10:1–21—A Lesson about Shepherding?

Before we conclude about the meaning of this story, we must make another observation about what the author was communicating with the facts of this story. Not many popular interpreters notice that the author puts two different events together in the shepherd sermon. 10:22 gives another occasion where Jesus talked about the shepherd. This, like the Feast of the Tabernacle (7:2), is another Jewish holiday called the Feast of Dedication (10:22). The time between 10:21 and 10:22 is around three months.

Why did the author present two clearly different historical occasions together in one theme of the shepherd? Is it not to resolve the problem of ritual and the religious institution represented by the temple? This brings us to the same problem of institutionalized religion and tradition the author had been dealing with all along. This section brings us to the fifth "I am" saying where Jesus is both the door and the good shepherd (10:7, 11). The author brought together two stories in a seamless manner in order to deal with the same topic. It would be good to take these stories as a single story, but it even better to treat them as two sermons combined into one in order to make a single point about religious traditions.

Another observation I need to make here is how the narrative plot of the shepherd sermon functions as preparation for the Lazarus story. If we read 10:3–5 carefully, Jesus talked about the shepherd's voice calling out his sheep. In 11:43, the same word "voice" also occurs in Jesus calling out Lazarus who recognized his voice and came out of the grave. Based on the way John told these stories, Lazarus's resurrection became the foretaste of every sheep's resurrection. The author wanted to show that Jesus' sermon was not an empty promise but could easily be a present reality. Lazarus represents the sheep who know Jesus. His resurrection foretold a great future for Jesus' followers.

A final observation I wish to make is the relationship between the shepherd sermon and the narrative containing the washing of the disciples' feet. In relation to the previous chapters, Jesus' action particularly relates well with John 10, where he gave the shepherd sermon. The Greek word for "take off" in 13:4 is the same as "lay down" in 10:11, 15, 17, 18. The Greek word for "put on" in 13:12 is the same as "take up" in 10:18. All the actions Jesus said he would do are now the same actions done to the garment. By using the same vocabulary in John 10 and John 12, John showed that the garment was symbolic of Jesus' death and resurrection. It reveals the total control Jesus had in his self-sacrifice. The story itself also shows Jesus' sovereignty, much like the shepherd king YHWH in the Old Testament.

Jesus made a prediction of his betrayal once again so that all those who follow will believe him (13:21–27). Thus, both the prior description of the author and the present sayings of Jesus confirm the intentional death Jesus was about to suffer. His action was willful and his timing impeccable. Unlike other martyrs, Jesus' death was under his exact control. The shepherd showed his sovereignty by giving up his life. Death was victory.

What then is Jesus' conclusion? The section of 10:37–38 shows that their mistake is their separation of the signs (10:33) from Jesus' claim. The signs verified the claim. The same problem happened three months earlier in 9:30–33. The word "know" occurs twice in 10:38. John's Jesus was making one important point: the event of insight should keep the person seeking more knowledge. Knowing is not about religious ritualism. Knowing is about having a relationship with the shepherd by listening to his voice. Why listen to his voice? It is because he is sovereign, in control of life itself.

Now that we have gathered the general meaning of the shepherd sermon, we must also look at how it fits into the larger context of John, before we decide the impact of this sermon and its meaning within the entire book. Jesus' response was specific to the temple context, especially in the latter part of the sermon. When reading John, the temple context is very strong and clear even at the start of Jesus' ministry. Most certainly, the temple theme is explicit here (as in John 2) because the Feast of Dedication in 10:22 was especially devoted to the temple. After all, Feast of Dedication (also known as Hanukah) was to commemorate the cleansing of the temple by the Maccebeans in their struggle against Antiochus Epiphanes. John 2 has already introduced the theme of cleansing, showing Jesus as the new temple. While the human effort to cleanse the temple failed, Jesus the New Temple would do what human political strength could not. The combined temple theme continues to attack the traditional religious institution. By showing himself to be the temple, Jesus then transformed the old building into something living and new. This could only be understood after the resurrection as stated in 2:22. As we may recall, the context of John 10–11 is also a discussion of resurrection. John's meaning is no coincidence. Jesus' full role as a transformed temple became clear after and not before his resurrection. Without the resurrection, none of the sermon would have made sense. Jesus became the stark contrast against the impotent temple and its rituals. This addresses the problem of the religious leaders in the blind man story. They were leading people to the earthly temple while Jesus became the true temple for the blind man to enter to meet God. 10:9 clearly states that Jesus led his people to the

Father. Jesus tended to mix his metaphors because the simplicity of a single metaphor was inadequate to describe his role.

Is there any reason to commend the shepherd sermon's popular interpretation at all? If we combine the sermon with Jesus' later reinstatement of Peter, we might answer, "Perhaps." Peter was commissioned by Jesus to become a shepherd of both sheep and lambs in John 21. We may not however interpret it in a loose and general way. The shepherd sermon is still not a manual to pastors. Rather, it illuminates the special authority of Jesus that he later passed down to Peter. Peter then took over Jesus' role after the resurrection, not in every sense, but in caring for the faith community who believed in the resurrection. The sermon then predicates Peter's duties. Like Jesus, Peter also would encounter conflicts with religious authorities after Jesus left. Jesus even hinted at the conflict in 21:18. If we link the two together, we may only see Jesus' authority and grace by giving Peter a second chance (and not make ourselves Peter).

In light of Jesus' society, conflicts were inevitable because what Jesus taught did not cohere with societal standard of honor and shame. While society disliked those who were crippled and rejected them, Jesus embraced them and made them full community members. Those who acted as thieves and robbers were in fact the elite of that community. Jesus' contrarian vision was to establish a new order and new leadership so that the dysfunction of his society would cease, replaced by the new order under his leadership (i.e., leadership of the Good Shepherd). The tension between community of the messiah and Israel's community would continue to mount in Jesus' time and in John's.

## APPLICATION

In the application of this passage, John communicated a great deal about Christ. Since the shepherd story is sandwiched between the healing of the blind man and the rise of Lazarus, the chapter functions in several ways. First, it works to transition the healing story into the resurrection of Lazarus. Second, in so doing, the author was arguing his case for Christ in a convincing way from a healing of a blind man—an impossible task in and of itself—into the revolutionary resurrection of Lazarus. By creating a transition between the blind man and Lazarus, the story speeds up the pace towards the cross where the shepherd will give and take up his life for the sheep. Since the idea of "life" is so prominent in this sermon, this sermon turns our attention back to life as stated already in 1:4. John's construction of this story lines up well with the entire narrative of the Gospel, beginning in John 1. Third, the way the plot includes a discussion on a Jewish festival links this chapter with every other Jewish festival in John. John wanted his believing community to rely solely on Jesus for the life they now lived, instead of focusing on rituals like their religious leaders did. Rituals can inhibit abundant life. At times, false religious leaders (bad shepherds) can use rituals and traditions to control the sheep. John's story warns of such danger.

In today's community of faith, rituals can become meaningful to some people. However, when rituals and certain "ways we've always done this" saturate the community, the community no longer represents the shepherd. Instead, it functions like the Pharisees who were more concerned with the rites than with their meaning. Rites, then, veil the glory and freedom that the true shepherd brings.

In this study, Jesus condemned the powerful, rather than siding with them. Quite often, within the faith community, the voice of reason and truth does not come from the majority view. Neither does it originate from the few powerful oligarchs. Jesus' action broke up the power structure. In our evangelical community, the powerful often dictate the trends. The masses merely follow the powerful or, worse yet, the popular. Jesus' action shows that we need to hear the minority voice, in this case, his voice. Truth may come out of the least expected places while the most obvious (though not all) leaders of these communities turn out to be "thieves and robbers." Uncritical acceptance of popular understanding on the one hand, and fearful submission to the powerful dictators on the other, both harm true faith. Every interpretive theory and every leader deserve close scrutiny.

## MISTAKES TO AVOID

Readers of Scripture will do well to simply ignore many of the given chapter divisions, which are not part of the original text. This passage has a clear meaning that has been skewed by a poorly chosen chapter division. The best thing the modern interpreter can do sometimes is to search for how the original undivided text naturally divides.

Another mistake people can make, which is closely related to the above discussion, is to ignore the narrative context of a sermon. Over and over again in this study, we have found that the narrative context has everything to do with what follows. If we ignore the narrative plot and assign our own meanings to the text, we do great violence to its meaning. Yet, there are cases when even dealing with the immediate narrative context is not quite enough, due to repeated themes throughout a given book (e.g., the temple theme in John). In the case of John's Gospel, the entire book is structured as one large narrative.

Another mistake people make is to assign a preconceived genre to the text. Quite often, people view the shepherd's story as a parable. Due to the symbolism of this shepherd saying, its genre goes beyond mere parable into true allegory. Allegories normally assign symbolic values to each character (e.g., the thieves symbolize the religious leaders, etc.). I have been taught for years that this is merely a parable. The difference between allegory and parable is that the latter does not assign symbolism to characters within the story while the former does. I suspect people do not want to see allegory as a legitimate category because they are afraid that someone will accuse them of allegorical interpretation. Yet, if the genre is allegory, we are merely "literally" interpreting it according to the internal logic of the narrative. There's nothing allegorical about the interpretation. Allegories can be understood in a straightforward and literal manner. I suggest that we need to determine genre by looking at what the text is doing first before finally arriving at a label for genre. As we have seen, the symbolic elements in the shepherd sermon make it an allegory where the characters have specific symbolic referents.

## DISCUSSION QUESTIONS

- What is the problem with the popular understanding of John 10?
- Who was Jesus referring to when he talked about those who came before him?
- How do we know that Jesus was not condemning the prophets who came before him?
- What issues come up when we read the entire narrative in light of John 9?
- What does this shepherd allegory teach us about our faith?

# PART TWO

Popularly Misused Texts in Letters

# 14

# Romans 8:28—
# All Things Work Out?

And we know that in all things God works for the good of those who love him,
 who have been called according to his purpose.

### THE POPULAR MEANING

A Calvinist and an Arminian stumble down a stair. The Calvinist says, "Whew, I'm glad that's over with." The Arminian says, "Whew, I've got to be more careful next time." How do things work out in this life? Romans 8:28 seems to provide the answer. Romans 8:28 is often used by Christians to encourage one another. It gives the sense that somehow things will work themselves out. Some even think that after becoming Christian, problems may magically go away as God's blessings shower upon the believer. All this sounds good and comforting, but we shall see that this is not supported by the text at all.

### WHERE DOES THE PASSAGE BEGIN?

Romans 8:28 belongs to the context of Romans 7–8. Typically, commentators rightly see chapter 8 as a follow-up solution to the problem of the law and flesh described in chapter 7. This way of dividing should not cause too many objections.

Since this is the first discussion about letters, let's briefly overview some of the important features in Paul's letters that will help give us an informed way of dividing the topics in sections. There are many ways for scholars to divide up a letter. Typically, words such as "therefore," "however," and "now" in our translations are very important indicators. Especially important for many scholars are the occurrences of "now" (e.g., 3:21; 8:1). Another common signal of division is the shift from third person description to second person address (e.g., 6:1; 8:1). These are simple features to keep in mind when we try to notice Paul's complex thoughts moving from one topic to the next. Let me just briefly outline the big picture of Romans 7–8 below.

| 7:1–6 | death and marriage illustration |
|---|---|
| 7:7–25 | individual's failed effort to obey the law |
| 8:1–11 | law of the Spirit overcoming the flesh |
| 8:12–17 | ethics of the Spirit |
| 8:18–38 | future hope and present plight for the Spirit community |

In addition to the above general observation, we can also determine that 8:1 is a new section in contrast to the entire chapter 7 with the dividing word "now" in 8:1. There is also a "therefore" at the front of 8:1. This "therefore" is yet another indicator of a dividing point.

One final thing we can notice to understand the division of the passage is Paul's usage of Greek independent clauses. For readers who do not know Greek, they can consult a good commentary for greater illumination of this point. But the Greek sentence structure suggests that 8:26–27 concludes the previous thought and 8:28 is a single sentence expressing a single thought. Certainly, having this knowledge is helpful. We are now ready to tackle this pivotal verse.

## THE MEANING OF THE PASSAGE

Before we understand the passage, it is important to find out the purpose of Romans as a whole. It seems that Romans is no mere theological treatise. Rather, like any ancient letter, its content was meant to propel the audience towards some action or ideology. We should attempt to make some kind of baseline projection of what purpose Paul might have been trying to accomplish in writing this letter.

*Romans 8:28—All Things Work Out?*

There ought to be no departure from the following consistent, threefold interpretive paradigm when looking for the purpose of Romans. First, the author may have made explicit statements about the circumstances from which he wrote. Second, the structure of the letter could lend itself to finding Paul's purpose. Third, the background of the audience who lived under imperial Rome could tie into the author's purpose for writing.

First, Paul had most certainly made clear that he wanted to travel to Rome many times. His wish to see the audience was clear (1:11). He wished to build that relationship at the present moment mainly because he needed the Roman Christians to provide a springboard for his mission to Spain (15:28). Whether Paul finally made it to Spain is not important. His purpose at the time was to reach Spain via Rome.

Second, the format of Paul's letter clearly confirmed Paul's purpose. In recent New Testament scholarship, the structure of Pauline letter writing has been found to contain many consistent features. Many scholars have observed that the prologues and epilogues of Paul's letters not only provide information about Paul's relationship with the readers, but also provide insights as to why Paul wrote. In other words, the prologue is there to establish the body of the letter. The prologue must be clear and simple in order to draw the attention of the listener. Thus, the prologue either reveals the intention of the author or prepares the listeners for the content of the writing. The same can be said of the epilogue. The epilogue reminds the audience, (in case they forget) of the author's topics and intentions. As a rule, I think each modern interpreter of Paul would do well to observe this feature with utmost attention. From the prologue in 1:1–17 and the extensive epilogue in 15:14–33, Paul made quite clear his missionary purpose. At the very least, the structure of Paul's letter writing informs the interpreter that the letter has a mission focus, with an intention of stopping off at Rome in order to launch Paul's Spanish mission.

Third, the background of the Roman audience deserves some words. Why did Paul want to use Rome as a jumping off point? The background of the Romans will provide the answer, at least in part. Paul converted in or around AD 35. His first travel/mission was around AD 37 (Acts 13). His primary areas of activity were the Cilicia-Syrian areas in this period (AD 35–46). Around AD 49, as Paul was writing the Epistle of Galatians and starting his second mission, Claudius the emperor expelled Jews (especially Christian Jews) from the capital Rome (Acts 15:40; 18:2; cf. Suetonius, Claudius 25:4). Paul wrote the Thessalonian Epistles around AD 50. After

Claudius died, Nero became the emperor around AD 54, upon which his Jewish subjects were allowed to return. This explains why Romans 9–11 was written, to reconcile the returning Jewish believers with gentile believers. Paul's third mission lasted from the end of Claudius's reign to the beginning of Nero's reign (AD 52–57). It was about this time that Paul wrote Romans. Paul seemed to have first penned the Corinthian Epistles around AD 55–56, where he conducted mission as far as Macedonia. During the three months of wintering in Corinth (Acts 15:25–26) around AD 57, Paul wrote Romans. He returned to Jerusalem shortly thereafter for the purpose of funding the mother church. This is a brief glimpse of the period when Paul wrote Romans. The historical circumstances and letter prologue and epilogue demand that we read Romans not as a theological treatise but as a mission letter. We must now move on to our task of interpreting 8:28.

Romans 8:28 is a complicated verse because of some of the grammar involved. Normally, Christians do not quote the entire verse starting with "we know," but choose to quote the content starting with "all things." Not looking at the entire verse will further shipwreck interpretation.

There is no problem with understanding "we know." Paul was suggesting that the content of the verse was already common knowledge within the early church. What comes after is much more complicated than what our translation has smoothed out. The subject is not exactly clear in the verse.

The difficulty of this verse seems quite clear from the variants in ancient manuscripts. Some manuscripts supply "God" before "works." Such guesses are part of the interpretive solutions in the history of interpretation of this verse. Where then did the scribe guess that "God" would be the unmarked subject?

The best place to find the subject would be from 8:29 where "his son" is mentioned, clearly indicating "God's son." A few interpreters posit the subject to be the Spirit from 8:27. This seems less likely simply because the Spirit's job in 8:27 seems to be praying while God's job is to carry through his purpose in 8:27–28.

There are, then, two possible translations of this troublesome verse. First, we could translate it this way: "And we know that [God] causes all things to work for the good . . ." Second, we could translate it, "And we know that in all things God works for the good . . ." Neither translation has things working out by themselves. We must also note that things do not work out in accordance with our will. All things" working out for good can be a possibility when we look at the translation, but we must be careful to note that the community for whom all things work are believers who love God and are called according to God's purpose. "All things" should not be limitless in scope. The "all things" here within context may have something to do with present suffering (8.18) and its relationship with the future glory (8.17). Believers do not skip over suffering at all, but trust in greater hope God had stored up for them. We must see that God works things out for "the good." The definition of this goodness is found in 8:29: to be more like Jesus. Therefore, the verse has the basic meaning that God works things out for the good of the believer in order to conform the believer to Christ's image, with a view toward justification and glorification (8:30).

Now, we must fit this meaning back into the larger scheme of things. The previous unit in 8:26–27 talks about the Spirit's work in helping with the prayer of believers. Much of the discussion prior to these verses also talks about the Spirit's work. The Spirit then enables believers to overcome the problem of the flesh and the demand of the law.

Let me discuss Paul's word usage here before I launch into the discussion below. When reading Paul, his singulars and plurals have very specific usages. Unlike our English language, the "you" can be singular or plural because Paul's usage is quite specific. Sometimes our English "we" really means "I." Not so Paul! One example of Paul's specific usage is 7:7–25. Paul expressed individual struggles with the law with singular "I" in 7:7–25, even though that struggle is universal. His singular pronoun focuses his topic on the individual. In other contexts, Paul would mix his singulars and plurals also for specific purposes. In 8:16–17, which we shall discuss below, Paul showed one such case of mixture between a singular and plurals.

The context of Romans 8 is entirely corporate with its language focusing on the corporate community. By referring to the work of the Spirit in Romans 8, Paul was talking not about individual salvation or God's providence towards individual believers but about corporate participation. While I do not deny that Paul viewed individual salvation as important, Paul's usage of language paints a broader picture. Paul's language of justification was thoroughly dominated by plural pronouns from Romans 3–7. Paul cited cases that applied to whole communities (7:1–3). He did not say in 7:1, "So, my brothers, each of you also died to the law," but "you (plural in Greek) also died to the law. . . ." The Spirit's work is best experienced through the faith community because Paul's concept of the Spirit was corporate. For example, in 8:16–17, he did not say, "The Spirit himself testifies with each of our spirits that each one of us is God's child. Now if each one is

God's child, then ..." No! He wrote, "The Spirit himself (singular) testifies with our (plural) spirit (singular) that we are God's children. Now if we are children ..." Paul envisioned a mixed metaphor of body and household. In seeing a singular spirit dwelling in "our" community, Paul envisioned the body of Christ. In seeing multiple children under one Father, he envisioned a household working cooperatively under a single head.

The plural further contrasts strongly with the greater context of this section found in chapter 7. This contrast seems to be a deliberate device used by Paul. He was noting the struggle each individual has with the law, but celebrating that when this individual is incorporated into this Spirit community, the community together would work out their ethical problems.

In the broader context of Romans, 8:28 shows God's role in the salvation of the new community. Paul's missionary purpose, evident in Romans 1 and 15, demands that a clear definition of the new community be given. When the community prays with the Spirit to conform to God's standard, God works things so that the community can express the traits of Christ. Paul's purpose is practical for his mission to Rome (and Spain) and not some abstract philosophy about fate and providence. His concern was for the witness of the community. Without knowing their place in the grand scheme, the Roman believers would not be able to do their local mission using their witness, let alone support Paul in his mission to the unreached areas. By knowing that God works to help the community to be more like Christ, the church can then trust in God's faithfulness to make them a living witness. How that plays out will come into discussion in Romans 9–11.

## APPLICATION

The application of Romans 8:28 is not at all complicated. It is a text that cares deeply about what Paul wanted to do with his mission. Paul's concern for witness is real. People often talk about going to foreign mission fields without first fixing the local witness. Paul's concern was for the church to adhere to the image of Christ. By acknowledging the fact that God works things out for her good, the church can rejoice in good or bad times. Things may not work themselves out, but God will work things out.

The plural in the passage also informs us that community is very important. The Spirit's work, in our modern times, has been viewed primarily as some kind of personal subjective experience. The plural tells us that the Spirit works things out in community. It is important to have personal subjective experience affirmed by the community. The ultimate measurement is whether such an experience has shaped the Church into the image of God's Son. If so, then perhaps the Spirit was working. If not, I'm afraid it was merely subjective personal experience.

## MISTAKES TO AVOID

The first mistake to avoid once again is the false chapter division suggested by modern translations. When we keep the big picture together, such as Romans 7–8, we will find a lot of meaning in the verses in the chapter.

The second mistake to avoid is neglecting the difference between plural and singular in Paul. This is a very common problem that deserves serious consideration because many strange applications have come out of it. If this aspect of Pauline thought can be fully explored, many popular applications will receive helpful adjustment.

The third mistake to avoid is the bypassing of the letter's purpose when interpreting its parts. The discussion of Romans is related primarily to mission. Somehow, if our theological interpretation fails to link up with mission, we have missed something significant.

## DISCUSSION QUESTIONS

- What seems to have been Paul's concern when he wrote Romans 8?
- How does Romans 8 fit into the purpose of the entire book?
- What is the Pauline view of the Spirit's work in the wider context of Romans 8?
- Who causes all things to work together, and why does it matter?

# 15

# Romans 13—
# Absolute Obedience to an Unjust Government?

> Let everyone be subject to the governing authorities, for there is no authority except that which God has established. The authorities that exist have been established by God. Consequently, whoever rebels against the authority is rebelling against what God has instituted, and those who do so will bring judgment on themselves....

### THE POPULAR MEANING

I REMEMBER HEARING A lecture on Romans 13 during seminary in which the instructor commented, "Christians do not have the right to conduct revolutions." Surely, this is the case if we read the text plainly. In recent years, many pastors who lean towards those in power also advocate absolute obedience to government. As I'm writing these words, the US is in an election year. So, whom do we obey? Should we obey Obama or Romney? What if the elected official has an ideology contrary to our faith? What then? These are not easy questions to answer if we take Romans 13 in straight dosage. Therein lies the danger of reading the content without understanding the rhetoric and intent. Where Does the Passage Begin?

First and foremost, this section is part of 12:1—15:15. As is typical of Paul, as well as ancient rhetorical rule or letter writing convention, the section has a major theme arising from major clauses. I believe the passage 12:1–2 is the head of the section, as it signals a response to the gospel which Paul so lovingly laid out before his audience in order to enlist their support for his mission. Romans 13 is an intricate part of that picture. So, this section really shows the specific relationship between government and gospel mission. How, in fact, is this section related to previous and following chapters?

## THE MEANING OF THE PASSAGE

Some relevant background will illuminate and correct the misunderstanding of this passage. Paul did not exactly view the government as a hindrance to his mission, but it had the potential to be so. In keeping with his ethics, Paul here dealt with potential disharmony between new gospel system and the world system, while Romans 14 deals with potential disharmony between Jewish and gentile Christians. As I have stated briefly in my discussion about Paul's purpose for writing Romans, during Claudius's reign he expelled Jews, especially Jewish Christians from Rome around AD 49. By the time of Paul's writing, when Nero had become king, the Jews were allowed to return. With the returning Jewish Christians, Paul anticipated conflicts about food and rituals. Romans 13 deals with potential conflict between existing Roman government and the church. Romans 14 deals with the result of Claudius's edict as fallout from previous government. Political background, then, governs both Romans 13 and 14.

It is not accurate to say that Paul's gospel is either "for" or "against" the government. The rhetoric of 13:1–7 proves that Paul had a very realistic and balanced view of government, simply because he put his mission above all else. If we stop reading this section as some kind of command, and begin setting it against the background of Paul's mission to Spain, we will immediately get Paul's message. It is also important to keep in mind that this was written before Nero started his persecution. This is a kind of peacetime Christian political-missiological ethic. Thus, it is not correct merely to read this section in terms of a general Christian attitude towards government. Rather, we may go deeper to see the importance of mission in terms of how Christians should deal with the government.

In Paul's teaching, he started with his thesis in 13:1a for several reasons. First, according to 13:1–2, even if the government could not perfectly represent God, it did (imperfectly) represent God. Here in these verses, the hierarchy is very clear: God, government, believer. By stating his case this way, Paul showed that God was superior to all governmental forces. The hierarchy links well with 12:1–2. The believer may be required to relinquish his rights as a kind of sacrifice in order to demonstrate God's rule (12:1–2). It was in this context that obedience to government took place. Second, according to 13:3–4, government served God for the good of the people. The "sword" Paul spoke about was often worn by tax officers and magistrates as a symbol of justice. Taxation generally came in form of property tax and poll tax. Taxation and the tax officer reminded every Roman citizen of the power of the emperor. In 13:4, the government was called "an agent of wrath." In 1:18, "wrath" is used of God's justice. Thus, here is the irony. The sword is obviously also a symbol of Roman imperialism. Paul was quite willing to allow for Roman imperialism, if his long-term ambition for mission (cf. Romans 1 and 15) could be fulfilled. "Whatever benefits the Christian mission" should be the application we draw.

Paul finished the chapter with a discussion on love and hope. Why did Paul do this when he had already written about love in 12:9–21? Too few commentators try to answer this question. Some commentators point out that the goal of Romans 12–13 is to urge the audience to follow the love command. Yet, why not put all the love commands together at this point instead of separating? The answer can provide a clue into Paul's purpose.

This present section on love is no simple, general, or abstract love ethic. The teaching on love and other virtues here is not some moralistic, philosophical teaching without context. Its placement here is not arbitrary. Its odd placement demands an explanation. The easiest explanation to the above question is that he simply wanted to discuss love in the light of the church's public relations (including towards government) in 13:1–7. Let me prove my point further in Paul's discussion of the debt of love. It is quite important not to take Paul's language literally about not owing any debt to anyone. In his society, debt (whether monetary or personal favor) put one under the power of the patronage system. The lender of money had power over those to whom he lent. By making "love" the debt metaphor, Paul put everyone under the power of God and not of humans. The Roman society was a network of debts and favors. Here, the Christian only has one debt: the debt of love. It is also a specific application of the foundation laid in 12:9–21. The mention of "neighbor" here shows the context of mission and witness.

*Romans 13—Absolute Obedience to an Unjust Government?*

Paul cited Jesus' teachings to firm up his own ideas about love (cf. 13:8–9; Matthew 7:12; 13:9). These citations are part of the transformation Paul envisioned happening through his gospel in 12:1–2. The church had become Christ-like by obeying Christ in a sacrificial manner. Paul concluded in 13:11–14 by talking about the eschatological aspect of this love. He turned his attention to the Christian hope. He gave Christians reason to love. Hope and love are related. If there is no hope for the future, why in fact should the Christian focus on love? The reason Paul put this here is simple. Paul clearly recognized that the human system was imperfect, but Christ's system was perfect. Yet, Christ's kingdom was coming progressively near in 13:11. So, why not be optimistic with a view to mission? The Christian response was to be fully devoted to living a life of alertness.

Following his eschatological discussion, Paul then gave some proper specific responses to the Christian hope in 13:12–14. First, Paul encouraged the Roman Christians to put aside their old identity which included all kinds of sinful lifestyles in 13:12–13. Second, Paul told them to put on a new identity, leaving no provision for the flesh. Paul saw no ultimate identity in his earthly citizenship, but only in his heavenly citizenship. Such a citizenship must exhibit certain behavior to demonstrate the identity. Love is the perfect expression of that eschatological reality. The more a Christian loves, the more he shows that he knows there is a future hope, and the more he will show the superiority of the Christian system over the worldly system.

## APPLICATION

As a person conscious of the political forces in his society, Paul advocated neither democracy nor monarchy. He neither approved bloody revolution nor passive submission, per se. In his concern for his mission to Spain, all things political were associated with his eschatological perspective (i.e., his post-exile ideal) and missiological goal. In essence, he is an advocate of the progressive and spiritual theocracy that can fit under any and every society. He had the idea of another kingdom within this worldly kingdom. His concern has always been theocracy within the faith community (i.e., a different kingdom) whether through the future salvation of all Israel as in 11:26, or the present obedience of the believer. So long as the gospel could spread, Paul tolerated the existing form of government, no matter how imperfect it was. He wanted the government to be a help rather than a hindrance to his mission. And that requires the church to be wise (and even flexible) in dealing with government. Complicated political situations cause many to lament and wish for an international community that governs a worldwide just system where everyone can benefit and not suffer injustice. No such worldwide system exists because none is a messianic and eschatological system. Without a doubt, this system is futuristic but can at least be partially realized in this age. Mission is the means by which this system is proclaimed, giving humanity hope. That is essentially Paul's purpose. The application is not about the Christian's civil rights, but about furthering God's mission. Thus, the application is quite situational and must not be duplicated in a wooden manner.

Romans 13 is the best example of a Pauline call to a Christian public life. The love paradigm is not abstract, but concrete. It serves as a witness. The believer is well aware of the role of government and the public square when practicing love. The love Paul talked about was not done in isolation but alongside of other equally noble endeavors. Many modern interpreters of this chapter miss an obvious point: Paul understands how the Roman government works. Paul here was putting himself as the example of such knowledge in order to show that he qualified as a missionary who could handle tough political situations. Paul's Christianity was not a monastic retreat from the world. Rather, he sought to engage the world actively within its flawed system with his flawless gospel of divine grace so that there would be a limited redemption of creation, until the full redemption of Jesus' second coming.

Evangelicals have always felt the tension in these verses. Many who hold a rigid view of applying Scripture just simply transfer the text into their lives. This will not work because Paul's content has to match his intent. Paul wanted only one thing; he wanted his mission to go smoothly. His stipulation was a temporary (and even convenient) measure.

## MISTAKES TO AVOID

The first mistake to avoid is a wooden, literal reading of Pauline ethics. Principles are eternal, but practices are situational. The interpreter needs to look at each piece of rhetoric and see how it fits the greater picture, which must be found in the purpose of the letter.

The second mistake to avoid is reading Paul as if there were no historical background bearing on the letter, just because the text does not state any

*Romans 13—Absolute Obedience to an Unjust Government?*

explicit background. The best place to look for background is not merely Paul's own background, but more importantly, the audience's background in association with extra-biblical and biblical historical background. Paul was writing based on what the audience knew.

## DISCUSSION QUESTIONS

- What is wrong with the absolute application of Romans 13?
- What is the background that helps us interpret this chapter?
- Why did Paul talk about love again here, when he already talked about it in Romans 12?
- What was Paul's primary concern in Romans 13?
- What are some of the ways the church can apply Paul's principles in our society?

# 16

## 1 Corinthians 6:12–20— My Body, God's Temple?

"I have the right to do anything," you say—but not everything is beneficial. "I have the right to do anything"—but I will not be mastered by anything. You say, "Food for the stomach and the stomach for food, and God will destroy them both." The body, however, is not meant for sexual immorality but for the Lord, and the Lord for the body. By his power God raised the Lord from the dead, and he will raise us also. Do you not know that your bodies are members of Christ himself? Shall I then take the members of Christ and unite them with a prostitute? Never! Do you not know that he who unites himself with a prostitute is one with her in body? For it is said, "The two will become one flesh." But whoever is united with the Lord is one with him in spirit.

Flee from sexual immorality. All other sins a person commits are outside the body, but whoever sins sexually, sins against their own body. Do you not know that your bodies are temples of the Holy Spirit, who is in you, whom you have received from God? You are not your own; you were bought at a price. Therefore honor God with your bodies.

### THE POPULAR MEANING

A little boy raised his hand in Sunday school and asked, "What do you do when you're bullied in school?" The teacher said, "In 1 Corinthians 3:17,

*1 Corinthians 6:12-20—My Body, God's Temple?*

Paul wrote that if anyone destroys God's temple, then God would destroy him. Since your body is the temple of the Holy Spirit, then God would destroy the bully." The packaged answer sounds like a great promise from God, but it does not solve the boy's bully problem.

This is another popular passage with miles of misunderstandings. A common application for this passage is that since the body is a temple, the Christian should take care of the body and not damage it by drinking excessively or smoking. Some would go further by suggesting exercise to make the body healthier.

All the suggestions above are probably quite helpful, but I suggest by the following discussion that these meanings do not come from this passage. Paul's matter is much more serious than what is commonly understood.

## WHERE DOES THE PASSAGE BEGIN?

The passage appears to begin at 6:12 and ends at 6:20. This is generally correct, and is evidenced in the flow of the text by the way Paul concluded a normal statement, followed by a rebuttal statement starting with "but." At the same time, in a broader sense, we should see how 6:12-20 fits within the wider scope. It seems to me that the first part of 1 Corinthians (chapters 1-6) deal with two topics that Paul had heard from Chloe's people (1:11). The first topic Paul cared about seems to be a discussion on leadership, based on a definition of wisdom in chapters 1-4. The second part to which our present text belongs is chapters 5-6 where Paul discussed a problem of making proper judgments. The best hint of a section division is 5:1, where Paul said, "It is actually reported" that there were some troubles. Thus, 6:12-20 belongs to this section about the trouble of making poor judgments.

## THE MEANING OF THE PASSAGE

Based on the above assessment of passage division, it is not hard to see what Paul was trying to do.

We should first examine 6:12-20 before looking broader for how these verses address the perceived problem. If we are to divide the passage up, we can say that it deals with two topics: the problem of Christian freedom (6:12-14) and the principle of Christian freedom (6:15-20). The problem of Christian freedom then is addressed by the principle Christian freedom.

Right Texts, Wrong Meanings

The verses in question that we need to understand are 6.15 and 6.19. The key concepts we need to deal with has to do with the word "body."

Some translations lead readers to generally understand 6:15 and 6:19 to be talking about the same thing. They are not. 6:15 has plural "bodies" followed by "members." The verb "is" that joins "bodies" and "members" is singular, however. A literal translation of 6:15 would look something like this:

> Do you know that your bodies (plural) are (should be "is") members (plural) of Christ himself?

Paul's grammatical construction is very curious because normally in Greek, the noun and verb match in terms of plural and singular. It seems that in this case, Paul had gotten his singular and plural mixed up. The English translation has harmonized the numbers for Paul, but such harmonization has diminished the force of Paul's thought. The reason Paul did this was to show all the members being linked together in their diverse ways in Christ. More curious is 6:15b where the members (plural) join together with a prostitute (singular). Was the entire church having sexual relationship with one woman all at once? Not likely. I think Paul was saying that even if a few members or one member had sex with a prostitute, it would corrupt the whole body of Christ.

The next verse in question is 6:19. The word "body" is singular but "you" is plural. It looks something like this:

> Do you (plural) not know that your (plural) body (singular) is a temple (singular) of the Holy Spirit, who is in you (plural), whom you (plural) have received from God?

If the "body" is the human body, it should be in plural "bodies." The singular body matches with another singular in this verse: the temple of the Spirit. Paul did not say, "Your bodies are temples." This mixture of number once again illustrates Paul's theological precision. The body here is not talking about human body. It is talking about the body of Christ that happens to be the temple (singular) of the Spirit. If each Christian's body is an individual temple, then Paul would use a plural "temples," but he did not. So, the verse is not about human bodies but Christ's body.

What can be said from these variations in Paul's language? There is a clear division within 6:15–20 where the variations occur. The switch is at 6:19 where Paul began a new sentence. From 6:15–18, Paul was suggesting illicit sexual relations can be equated to letting every member of Christ's body have sex with a single prostitute. Even if there is only one case, the church has already been defiled. Paul was borrowing from his Jewish ethics in dealing with the Corinthian situation. After all, gentiles went to prostitutes and mistresses all the time. Paul did not say how a single prostitute would defile the body. Perhaps a few of the members were taking turn going to a single prostitute and started influencing others in their morality. This may be our best guess, but Paul did assume that this would defile the body because each member is joined to Christ (6:16–17). That much is clear.

Chapter 6:19–20 begins another section because it moves argument from negative into positive. While having impure relationships defiles other members of Christ's body, Paul now restated the nature of this body by a metaphor of the Temple. This same temple was bought by God, according to 6:20.

What then was Paul dealing with? If we take the first issue mentioned in 6:12, we get some sense of what challenged him. Paul used "but" to refute the same mentality expressed in two opposite ways. The first part, before the "but," was something that the Corinthians used as motto in their abuse of Christian freedom. Thus, not every sentence originated from Paul, but Paul quoted from others. In the sayings of 6:12–13, Paul wanted to point out, first, that not everything is beneficial; second, that some things can master the believer; and third, that fulfillment of the flesh is temporary.

So, Paul's usage of the prostitution example has all three points in mind, as the topic is used to address them. In other words, going to a prostitute would be unbeneficial, potentially addictive, and would focus the believer on temporal things. This is the starting point where Paul drew up the two metaphors: body and temple. Now we must look at the impact this passage has in the entire section of chapters 5–6. In order to do this, we must appreciate the argumentation leading up to 6:12–20.

Heading up 5:1 is the topic of immorality. The word used here includes sex outside of marital covenant. The sexual deviance suits the later discussion about sexual immorality very well. Paul condemned them because the Corinthians were proud of what they had done. There was a serious lapse of judgment. This leads to the next controversy in 6:1–11 where a different lapse of judgment took place with a law suit. It seems that the thread that ties immorality and law suit together is judgment. We must notice why I say judgment for the sexual case. Paul not only condemned the immoral couple but he further condemned the bragging of the Corinthians about their tolerance. While they tolerated what they should not have, they also became intolerant of one another's differences leading to a public suit. How, then, would the suit be related to 6:12–20? I think it is because the suit breaks up the body of Christ.

Thus the body principle does not merely have a moral dimension. It rather ties up the entire chapters 5–6 into a kind of principle of unity. Anything that breaks up unity, whether it is a huge trespass like immorality or a small trespass like one brother taking advantage of another, is wrong. It is therefore easy to see how 6:12–21 is more than a moral lesson. It is a theological lesson about the unity of the body.

We have to look even broader to see what came before chapters 5–6 in order to gain an understanding of how 6:12–20 fits into the overall discussion of this letter. The problem of wisdom in chapters 1–4 definitely involves some disunity, especially with people claiming to belong to this or that party (in 1:12). So, the Corinthians were not correct in their definition of wisdom, thus leading to big conflict. If we link this up, we can certainly see 6:12–20 not only as the conclusion to chapters 5–6, but as a grand conclusion for chapters 1–6, the first part of the book, before moving on to the second part of the book staring in chapter 7.

If we look even more broadly at the historical background of "the body" as a metaphor, Paul's usage was quite in line with his contemporaries. "Body" can be used to describe political entities. In other words, each political body had a function and identity. If Paul was discussing not only Christ's body (as a theological-soteriological term) but also was including the idea of an organized human effort (as a political term), then the problem is not merely theological or ritual but has to do with the identity and function of the church in the world. The messianic kingdom should contrast with the worldly system. Otherwise, the witness would be lost. The real question is this: what kind of identity and function does the church have in society?

## APPLICATION

The proper application of this passage most likely varies a bit from the moralistic, popular application. While there is a moral dimension to this passage, Paul was using morality to deal with a much broader issue. Unity remains the thread throughout 1 Corinthians. Paul's big concern was unity, and not in the way we imagine, either.

In Corinth, there were things that the Corinthians needed to become strict about (i.e., moral purity) that they were letting slide. There were other

*1 Corinthians 6:12-20—My Body, God's Temple?*

things they needed to let go of, but were quite strict about (i.e., ego-based conflicts). Therein lies the problem. The Corinthians did not have the true wisdom needed to know what their priorities should be. Paul was not dealing with immorality only. He was dealing with immaturity.

What then broke up Christ's church? I dare to suggest a lack of sound judgment about what is important and what is not. I think it is important to address the moral question, but it is even more challenging for a church to address the maturity problem. A church can be perfectly moral yet immature. I think maturity takes longer than moralistic motto of "do this . . . don't do that." Therefore, we need to use the moral discussion of Paul's as a starting point, but not as a finishing point. We have our own context. Although we may be quite an immoral group, we may have other equally insidious problems in our churches that put us off balance, resulting in the breaking up of the church. Most people, church leaders included, have only understood Paul at the wooden, literal level, but if we read the entire argumentation from chapters 5–6, we will surely gain a broader perspective.

What kind of issues can break up the body of Christ? According what we have seen, two misjudgments will lead to this disaster. First, a misjudgment about morality can cause such breakup. Second, the mishandling of interpersonal differences can also destroy unity. We must notice that Paul was dealing with Christians and not non-Christians. He had no expectation for non-Christians. In fact, he assumed that non-Christians lived by a different moral standard (5:1). His expectation was for Christians. Church conflicts should be solved justly, openly, and sensitively, knowing that the unity of Christ's body is at stake. More importantly, the church's identity and function are at stake, especially relating to her witness.

## MISTAKES TO AVOID

The first mistake to avoid is treating Paul's teachings as separate sections without relating them to one another. This is a very serious mistake because it leads to a kind of Christian legalism that sounds highly moralistic, yet is desperately irrelevant and inflexible.

The second mistake to avoid is failing to link a passage with the book's overall purpose, sometimes accessible at the beginning of the book. Those who do regular inductive Bible study often commit this mistake because it is easy to isolate a unit without caring for the whole context. As the beginning of 1 Corinthians has already indicated, Paul was deeply concerned with unity. This theme continues to be relevant the rest of the book.

## DISCUSSION QUESTIONS

- What is the problem with the popular interpretation?
- What difference do the singulars and plurals make in the interpretation of these verses?
- What was Paul's purpose in writing these verses?
- What is the relationship between maturity and morality?
- How is Paul's teaching applicable to our churches today?

# 17

# 1 Corinthians 11:1—
# Imitate Paul, Imitate Christ?

Follow my example, as I follow the example of Christ.

### THE POPULAR MEANING

PREACHERS OFTEN USE 1 Corinthians 11:1 rhetorically, to add to the force of their sermons. Then, I've heard the more pious objection of, "Why not just imitate Christ directly?" The most general and popular meaning of 1 Corinthians 11:1 is that Paul was trying to get people to imitate him. A more specific understanding is to see Paul asking people to imitate his way of imitating Christ. Yet, the ethics of imitation of Christ present great difficulties because of their general nature. Even if we assume imitation of Christ being legitimate, in what way should a Christian imitate Christ? There is no certain answer to this difficult question. It is therefore important to find out what Paul meant exactly, in order to apply this verse in the right context.

### WHERE DOES THE PASSAGE BEGIN?

First Corinthians 11:1 belongs to a greater section starting from 7:1, where Paul started dealing with the matter about which the Corinthians wrote him (cf. 7:1, 25; 8:1, 4; 12:1; 16:1, 12). Within the greater scheme of things, the section 7:1—11:1 deals with some specific issues in a highly logical manner. Paul started the section with a discussion on the neutral issue of marital freedom in chapter 7. The next topic is a grey area of idol meat in chapter 8. Chapter 9 discusses Paul's proper use of freedom and how it will impact a believer's reward. Chapter 10 talks about Israel's mistake.

The section 10:14—11:1 is the smallest unit to analyze for the purpose of the present exercise, as it contains a kind of saying at 10:23 that Paul swiftly addressed. We should look at the basic meaning from the small unit before looking at the impact of this verse for the entire section.

## THE MEANING OF THE PASSAGE

We start at 10:14—11:1. In the middle of this discussion about idol meat is 10:23. The saying found here is in the same format as all the other sayings in 1 Corinthians (cf. 6:12). This repetition of "everything is permissible" seems to be a kind of motto the Corinthians lived by as a result of a hedonistic understanding of Paul's free gospel. This is one more correction from Paul.

The problem here is quite simple. The Corinthians were struggling with eating idol meat. Paul wanted to give them principles to deal with the struggle. Paul made his argument starting with the Lord's Supper in 10:16-17 and contrasting it with idol feasts in 10:18. In contrasting, he showed how incompatible the Lord's Supper is with idol feasts (this is given a more elaborate discussion in 10:19-22).

In his argument this far, Paul had used a rich variety of words to describe the various elements of idol worshipping. First, Paul used the general term "idolatry," having to do with the whole of idolatry in 10:14. Then, in using a different term, "sacrifices," he talked specifically about the thing that was being used in the sacrificial ceremony in 10:18. Furthermore, Paul used a more specific term translated "a sacrifice offered to an idol" to describe the sacrificial meat in 10:19. This third term is more technical, denoting a piece of meat that was to have one part burnt, another part eaten in the temple feast, and the last part sold in the market. Without a doubt, the discussion of 10:20-22 is discussing the part of the ceremony, allowing the worshipper to eat the meat. Finally, Paul used another term, "offered in sacrifice," in 10:28 to describe meat sold in the market. If we do not distinguish the different words, Paul would seem to be contradicting himself because it seems that he disallowed for any kind of eating in 10:14-22 while he allowed conditional eating in 10:23-33.

The reason Paul had two seemingly contradictory suggestions is because of two different scenarios. The first scenario, from 10:14–22, is talking about the eating ceremony in the temple. The second scenario, from 10:23–33, is talking about the eating of the market meat at home. The condition for eating is very specific. Restraint from eating occurred only when a person with a questionable conscience mentioned that the meat was bought from the market where temple meat was sold in 10:28. Scholars have argued long and hard about whether this person was a weak believer or a non-believer. Paul cast his net among the widest in 10:32, which includes unbelieving Jews and Greeks, as well as the church. How can an unbeliever stumble? Perhaps, he would have further misunderstanding about the Christian faith (whatever it was) that could never be clarified at the moment. The same misunderstanding would prevent him from coming to faith. So, for Paul, he suggested restraint all of the time when the eating was directly involved with idolatrous ceremonies. Outside of the temple, he was quite free and gave conditions under which eating or restraint could take place due to the condition of the marketplace. Idol meat was everywhere. Unless one wanted to be a vegetarian for the Lord, a lot of good meat would come from the temple.

The overarching principle is the stumbling of the weak one (10:31–32). The weak in conscience might just stumble (10:32). As long as no one stumbled, eating meat outside of the temple was permitted. We must notice that Paul was dealing not so much with those who wanted to restrict others' freedom. Paul was not calling for restriction any time someone suggested that perhaps someone might stumble. He was actually talking about someone who really had a questionable conscience telling the strong that there was a problem. With this in mind, we must understand Paul to be saying that the strong one had responsibility to understand who the weak ones were. This would put the burden on the strong one, including Paul himself.

With the stumbling principle in mind, Paul used his own example of pleasing others for the sake of their salvation in 10:33. Paul was here talking about his mission to save all, including Jews and Greeks. He sacrificed his own habits to bring salvation to these groups, which brings us to 11:1. What then does this say about 11:1? It is not a general statement. Paul imitated Christ in one thing, and that one thing is in 10:33. Paul's imitation therefore is the imitation of the missionary spirit of Jesus. Such a spirit requires sacrifice for the sake of others.

When we view all the topics together, it appears that chapter 7 belongs on its own with Paul using personal example to illustrate the freedom of choice on completely neutral issues. I use the term "neutral" in a very specific sense based on the discussion thus far. Neutral issues are not necessarily morally black and white issues, but may have black and white implications. The neutral issues in many cases might not cause any real spiritual stumbling, but can still contain danger. Then, chapters 8:1—11:1, to which 10:14—11:1 belong, ought to be read together to address issues with some consequences that may not be completely neutral.

From chapter 8, the word used for idol meat is descriptive of the food in the temple (8:1, 4, 7, 10) also found in 10:19. The Corinthians probably got into the temple to participate in pagan feasts. They had written Paul about this, and Paul sought to answer them. If we want to compare chapters 8 and 10, we can see that Paul added one existing condition, not within the temple, but outside of it in the marketplace. We can see that Paul was especially careful to creating enough nuances to fit his gospel of freedom. He did not give their question a merely negative and simplistic answer. To answer chapter 8, Paul also used his personal example in chapter 9 and Israel's example in 10:1–13. His example has to do with giving up one's knowledge and rights for the sake of the gospel. Israel's example has to do with the nature of God's people in their worship. This fits nicely for Paul to close in 10:14—11:1 with a more nuanced scenario. The principle however remains the same: seek the good of others even if it means giving up one's own rights. That is his imitation of Jesus Christ. As a result, he could accomplish the unity among Corinthians which he so desired, as he stated at the start of 1 Corinthians. The individual interest should give way to the greater good, not just any kind of greater good, but in purity, unity, and witness.

## APPLICATION

As we can see, Paul's application is not a general imitation of Jesus Christ in every regard. Rather, he was talking about a certain ministry of Christ, namely the self-sacrifice needed to help others to participate in salvation. Thus, if Paul was referring to Jesus' sacrifice, then any other kind of sacrifice would pale in comparison. In other words, Paul was arguing from the smaller issue of giving up certain food to the greater example of giving up one's life (i.e., Christ's sacrifice). The argument moves from lesser to greater.

*1 Corinthians 11:1—Imitate Paul, Imitate Christ?*

The issue of idol meat seems to be concerned not with the meat itself, because it is just a piece of meat. Rather, Paul's issue is bigger. He wanted to look at how such practices cohere with or violate the Christian faith and edification. Paul used a symbol from the Lord's Supper in two ways. First, it denotes the unity of the body. Second, it denotes a kind of purity in the participation of the meal, that shows a new life within the Christian. Eating the meat at home while causing the weak person to stumble violates the first meaning of unity, while eating in the temple violates the second meaning of sacred purity.

Now, not every church struggles with idol meat these days. Even if in some instances there are struggles, Paul's application seems very easy. When I taught in Asia, this issue is quite contentious because of the widespread practice of local religions; such arguments tend to get quite passionate. In the West, this issue seems non-existent unless we understand that Paul was really dealing with grey areas of every culture. However, every church faces some grey issue one time or another. Whatever it is, Paul's basic premise is this. As long as people are not stumbled, everything is permissible. This demands that believers must be sensitive to the people around them. This demands that brothers and sisters know one another in a deep way. Unity is hard work. While Paul respected personal rights, he especially favored the rights of the weak ones. Christian life then, is not about personal rights as much as it is about unity with the weak ones.

We must be careful to recognize that Paul was not suggesting so much caution that Christians should stop doing something every time someone says that a weak one might stumble. In our churches, many would say generally, "Someone will stumble," in order to accomplish their own agenda. Paul was not in favor of such spiritual hijacking. Rather, Paul would want the weak ones to voice their spiritual weaknesses for others to discuss so that all involved can think through the best plan of action. Verbal communication is necessary for unity to happen. Therefore, the popular idea that the strong one is responsible for the entire problem is only half true, at best. The weak one must also bear some responsibility to admit his weakness. Thus, application should point to issues of unity, communication, sensitivity, and edification.

## MISTAKES TO AVOID

The first mistake is obvious. If we take Paul's statements as general truth, we shall create questions we cannot answer. 11:1 is the perfect example. When encountering such a proverbial saying as 11:1, there is a huge temptation to generalize the Christian life in one particular way, especially if its rhetorical usage brings strong impact on the audience of our sermons. We must resist because such a practice creates more problems than it solves.

In line with the previous text we discussed from 1 Corinthians, another mistake interpreters make is neglecting Paul's stated purpose right at the beginning. As I mentioned earlier, every letter tends to state its main purpose at the beginning. The importance of Paul's prologue is obvious within 1 Corinthians. The problem of disunity caused dispute over wisdom in 1 Corinthians 1:18—2:16, caused dispute over Paul's apostleship versus the authorities of others in 3:1—4:21, caused problems for dealing with disputes of various problems in 5:1—11:34, caused disputes over spiritual gifts in 12–14, and so on. Therefore, when unity is not the main theme, the interpretation will become problematic. It is in imitating Jesus in self-sacrifice that unity happens.

## DISCUSSION QUESTIONS

- What is wrong with the popular interpretation?
- Why is this teaching about imitating Jesus not only limited to idol worshipping cultures?
- What kind of neutral issues does the church face today?
- What are the responsibilities of the strong and the weak?
- What exactly would imitating Jesus look like in our modern culture?

# 18

## 2 Corinthians 6:14—
## Unequally Yoked, Unequally Married?

Do not be yoked together with unbelievers. For what do righteousness and wickedness have in common? Or what fellowship can light have with darkness?

### THE POPULAR MEANING

THIS IS ONE VERSE that has been set in stone for intermarriage between Christians and unbelievers. Whenever young people ask why they should not date people of different faiths or no faith, many of our Sunday school teachers or youth counselors quote this verse. The interpretation goes something like this: The Christian who marries a non-Christian will become unequally yoked. As we shall see, this interpretation is merely a smoke screen for denouncing inter-faith marriage. I'm not suggesting that there is no biblical warrant for such denouncement but is this really the case for this verse?

### WHERE DOES THE PASSAGE BEGIN?

Second Corinthians 6:14 appears to head the section of 6:14—7:1. Prior to this section, Paul was sharing about his ministry, in order to enlist greater support for his mission. Thus, we should look to clarify the meaning of this verse by what Paul said before and after it.

## THE MEANING OF THE PASSAGE

The meaning of this passage depends on the way we view 2 Corinthians. Without a doubt, getting the passage division is very important. We shall examine that first. From a macroscopic point of view, getting the purpose of the entire book is also important. We shall discuss it later after getting the general meaning of 6:14 in light of its immediate context.

Although 6:14 is not clear on its own, its meaning becomes increasingly clear in 6:15—7:1. This makes 6:14 the introduction to the content that follows. The examples that follow all have to do with the theme of idolatry. Starting from 6:14–16a, there are pairs of contrast, mostly having to do with pagan religion. As we may recall from the above discussion on idol meat, the Corinthians had the tendency to participate in pagan rites. Paul's concern for them had not diminished since the writing of 1 Corinthians. Especially important is the usage of the temple analogy in 6:16. This is not talking about an individual Christian as much as about the entire church. The plural "you" in 6:14 gives this fact away. Thus, Paul talked about religious purity in 6:19 using the same analogy we have discussed above in. The theological logic is the same.

More telling are the quotations from the Old Testament in 6:16b–18. The quotations are either strung together for rhetorical effect or drawn from familiar texts Paul had previously taught the Corinthians. Both possibilities are valid. 6:16 quotes from the purity code of Leviticus 26:12. Here is one area where Paul clearly showed how he translated the Old Testament purity code into his own ethics. Paul then quoted from either Isaiah 52:11 or Ezekiel 20:34, 41. I prefer to see it as a quotation from Isaiah simply because Paul uses Isaiah often elsewhere in his letters. His frequent usage of Isaiah shows that he had taught extensively from it to his audience during his gospel ministry. The Isaiah context seems to be talking about coming out of captivity. The resemblance from Ezekiel only suggests that perhaps Ezekiel was familiar with Isaiah's work or that he received the same message from YHWH while in exile. In 6:18, Paul quoted next from 2 Samuel 7:14.

Now we must discuss what the meaning of such a string of quotes is. Leviticus 26:12 is easy enough because it is a straightforward covenant context where YHWH gave a definition of what being his people meant. For Paul, the many Old Testament ritual texts had less relevance after the coming of the messiah, but this particular one remained true for his day because such action directly impacted the worship of YHWH himself. The worship of YHWH was part of the core of Paul's gospel. Isaiah 52:11 is

## 2 Corinthians 6:14—Unequally Yoked, Unequally Married?

equally straightforward in calling for exiles to return to God's promised land and depart from pagan exile. Second Samuel 7:14 appears to be trickier. The verse contains God's promise to David for his son Solomon. Paul here applied the verse to the church. The connection may that both are recipients of God's promise. I'm not sure whether the Corinthians actually understood this verse in its original context, as Paul did not make a habit of quoting from 2 Samuel in his letters. My best guess is that the first two quotes were familiar to the audience while the last one gives rhetorical effect. Perhaps if Paul had some Jewish readers, they would understand the last quote, but there is no evidence that the Corinthian church had many Jewish members. That said, the general theme of being God's people is unmistakable in all three quotes.

What can we summarize so far? Paul was dealing with some who were most likely getting mixed up with the practices of their former pagan lifestyle. He appealed to the Christian identity as God's people and the worship of YHWH to deter such practices. Such practicioners were in this specific religious sense, "unequally yoked" with the world. Paul emphasized this by talking about the uniqueness of Israel from her neighbors, quoting the three Old Testament verses we have discussed above. In case anyone misses Paul's point, 7:1 then talks about maintaining purity from impure religion that contaminates the church. We must now understand the passage in the light of book context.

How can we set the baseline for the macroscopic interpretation? The main theme or purpose of 2 Corinthians is notoriously difficult to nail. The letter seems to divide into two parts, chapters 1–9 and 10–13. The difficulty in analysis comes because the tone of chapters 1–9 is peaceful, while in 10–13 it is quite combative. However, even within relatively peaceful discussion, careful readers will find defensive rhetoric in 2.12–17 (e.g. "unlike so many" in 2.17) or reconciliatory rhetoric in 7.8–13 (i.e. the need to explain why changes were needed.) The original tension did not completely go away as Paul wrote 2 Corinthians 1–9. I presume that chapters 1–9 were written first before Paul got some bad news from his coworkers that unrest had once again taken over the church. Therefore, it is more sensible to understand what is said here in light of the text just prior to this context as well as the beginning of Paul's letter where his purpose may be found. The tone of the beginning of the letter seems peaceful enough, where Paul spent some time encouraging the Corinthians. Part of the discussion explained why Paul could not travel to Corinth for the moment. Therefore, 6:14—7:1

must be something that was on his mind, knowing that the Corinthians were prone to falling into their former pagan lifestyle. We can see Paul's exhortation for religions purity to be a reminder to the Corinthians. Paul's discussion in 6.14–7.1 seems to be an insertion between 6.12 and 7.2 where Paul's relationship with the Corinthians rather than idolatry is the topic. In fact, if we take out the section 6.14–7.1, the section would run smoother. No interpreter can avoid seeing 6.14–7.1 as an insertion.

What did these Corinthians have that would cause Paul to talk about unclean things, when surrounding context seems to be talking about having good will? Did Paul skip over a few logical steps? Unclearness can be the trouble with letters. They tend to be only part of the dialogue between author and readers. I do not think Paul skipped over a logical step.

The discussion 6.14-7.1 is not really about idolatry because the surrounding context has already indicated that it was about Paul's relationship with the Corinthians. Instead of making idolatry the issue, Paul was urging the Corinthians not to be in the company of those who would corrupt the church the way idolatry would corrupt the church. As such, Paul used idolatry as an analogy. Thus, the section was neither about marriage nor idolatry but about the kind of corrupting influence that could creep into the church, if the church did not watch out. Very likely the section 6.14–7.1 describes false teachers who had negative doctrinal and moral influences. Paul's analogy about idolatry then became a stern warning to the Corinthians. Paul perfectly (and most likely, strategically) inserted this harsh teaching in the midst of a discussion about good will. His was a clever ploy of persuasion.

With the above in mind, Paul's biographical details in 5:11—6:13 make sense. Paul strongly showed his dedication to his God and his ministry. Furthermore, he wrote with a mild tone to earn the good will of the Corinthians so that he could give the appropriate advice to them about a sensitive lifestyle issue.

## APPLICATION

We can see that the application of 6:14 is very tricky. For sure, it has nothing to do with marriage. If we want advice on marriage with unbelievers, we could look elsewhere, such as in 1 Corinthians 7:39. Nor is the message of 6:14 about not going into business with unbelievers, either. Paul had suggested elsewhere that believers can certainly hang around unbelievers (1 Corinthians 5:9–10).

Paul was suggesting that the Christian lifestyle should be compatible with Christian worship. The center of Paul's argument is about worship.

The idea of God's temple being the church is a fascinating case about Christian conduct. Paul had repeatedly used this analogy in his argument for various kinds of purity in the area of doctrine and moral. Here, Paul was not talking about eating idolatry but about the danger of bad company. The danger was so great that he likened it to idolatry. In his worldview, idolatry was a capital punishment. In other words, bad company was deadly in the ruination of the entire church. When looking at the topic Paul was addressing, his purpose was neither to stop marriage between believers and unbelievers nor to stop idolatry. Instead, he got at the root of the entire purity problem of the church. The church ought to be quite careful in the kind of teachers who could teach in it. By opening the church's embrace towards the apostle and his coworkers, the church would keep from the danger of being associated with false teachers whose crime would be as severe as idolaters.

I would suggest that we may, however, be able to apply this in terms of Paul's principles of purity and worship. There are many things in a Christian's former lifestyle that could prevent him from worshipping God. This is where believers need to pay attention. Lifestyle choices *can* impact our spirituality. Not only will they impact our individual spirituality, but our choices will also impact the wider church. I see once again Paul using the temple analogy to teach this truth. Many Christians think that their choices are small and individualistic, but the impact, according to Paul's analogy, has the potential to escalate into something quite large.

## MISTAKES TO AVOID

The first mistake is obvious. Christians apply verses at random apart from careful contextual consideration. Moreover, they often pick an area to apply where they're largely not personally affected. While Christians often quote this verse for marriage, I rarely see this being applied in business dealings or any other kind of social dealings. If we want to generalize a verse, we should then apply it in everything and not just a select few things that matter to us. Application to marriage with this verse is a clear example of using Scripture to push personal preferences and agendas.

The second mistake to avoid is neglecting the overall purpose of the book. The book's purpose is not as clear in 2 Corinthians as in 1 Corinthians.

## Right Texts, Wrong Meanings

Most likely, it is because the book was written over a longer period of time. Even so, understanding the purpose does not have to difficult. We not only noted the content of the first part of 2 Corinthians, but also the tone of the chapter. Paul's tone certainly gives us a hint as to what he meant in 6:14—7:1.

### DISCUSSION QUESTIONS

- What is wrong with the popular interpretation?
- What was Paul's concern?
- How would church life today reflect his concern?
- What mistake does the marital interpretation make?

# 19

# Ephesians 2:14—
# Which Wall?

For he himself is our peace, who has made the two groups one and has destroyed the barrier, the dividing wall of hostility....

**THE POPULAR MEANING**

THE WORST ABUSE OF this verse comes from a song I heard in church. It is based on this verse, which talks about our reconciled relationship with God and that Jesus has brought peace. The abuse comes from the quotation of this verse in the song. The peace the song talks about is more about a feeling of peace as a result of being right with God. Surely, the "feeling" of peace with our Creator may be the result of our salvation, but we cannot possibly derive that truth from this text.

Another meaning people make of it (and this is exclusive to many evangelical Christians) is that Jesus has given us a peaceful feeling in our hearts from his work. This special feature of evangelicalism saturates the songs evangelicals sing both in older hymns as well as contemporary worship songs. No doubt, Jesus might have brought some peace of mind to many believers, but the author of Ephesians was talking about anything but warm sentiments. As we shall see, the popular meanings above are as far as they are wide from the author's true meaning.

## WHERE DOES THE PASSAGE BEGIN?

As far as the division of Ephesians goes, the traditional dividing point at 2:1 is accurate. First, it is where the pronouns switch into second person plural. Second, the topic seems to have shifted. Yet, we need to consider a few things.

First, in all New Testament letters, the entire letter is heard from beginning to end. Therefore, every term must be defined by the way a term is used within the letter as a whole. Second, in a letter, one more factor clearly dictates the meaning: the background. Thus, what is it about the background of Ephesus that is important to know as we read the letter of Ephesians? Let us now briefly dwell on the second issue first. This will be brief.

First, the letter is like a lot of letters; it was the product of an oral society. As such, it was read aloud. All letters have personal touches, unless there are reasons not to have personal greetings. Ephesians is one such exception. Due to the lack of personal greetings, it was most likely a circular letter not only for Ephesus, but also for its neighbors in Asia Minor. Yet, we can use Ephesus as the starting point because of its importance. As the capital of Asia Minor, Ephesus served as the influencer of culture around that general area.

Second, we must consider the city of Ephesus. The church was originally founded by Paul in AD 53 according to Acts 19.[1] Paul visited again in AD 57. In terms of population density, Ephesus was second, behind only Rome itself, in the empire. If Asia Minor was a place of idolatry, Ephesus was the ultimate statement of that religious culture because of its famous Artemis worship. The Artemis temple itself is one of the ancient wonders of the world, with its size more than four times that of the Parthenon in Athens, taking 120 years to build. The temple, which was about six stories high in terms of modern buildings, was larger and wider than a modern football stadium. The attraction of the Artemis temple apparently brought additional wealth to the city, especially attested in the temple's own treasury. The importance of the temple was testified to by its function as a sanctuary for those who fled to it. Presumably, an attacker would respect the sanctity of the building. The temple offered salvation!

---

1. The authorship of Ephesians and also the Pastorals has been debated among scholars. It is not clear whether Paul wrote this letter or not. Thus, I use "author" instead of "Paul" sometimes, but the authorship problem will not hinder our present exercise.

In addition to the idolatrous environment, Ephesus had a political culture in Asia Minor, relying on Roman wealth. In Roman ideology, the king was the metaphorical head or father of the national family guided by a culture of honor and shame. The city sought political honor through loyalty to Caesar, evident in Augustus's dedication of a temple in the city to Julius Caesar. It was, then, a very political city as well as an idolatrous place. As early as Paul's first mission to Ephesus, Acts 19:35 shows the town clerk stating the honorary title of temple keeper for Ephesus. Part of the Ephesian architectural, political, and religious glory came from its Romanization under Augustus. After that, the city had a distinctly Roman characterization. Ephesus was a mini-Rome in Asia Minor. Paul's Asia Minor mission was clearly prominent in the Ephesian church, as the author of Acts 19 went into great details about its founding. We find in the letter both political and religious language combined, which certainly speaks to Asia Minor's Christianity.

## THE MEANING OF THE PASSAGE

The passage falls within the section about the change that came after Christ. From 2:1–10, the author plots out the origin of life changes. The language in 2:1–10 is supernatural (e.g., 2:1–2), psychological (e.g., 2:3), salvific (e.g., 2:4–5), eschatological (e.g., 2:6–7) and soteriological (2:8–10). 2:11–22 then talks about the result of God's work. In 2:14–15, the author was talking about a wall between Jews and gentiles, when he talks about the two humanities and the law. Although God had been doing all the work on humanity, there is no discussion about a wall between God and humanity in 2:14–15. What are the two parties separated by the wall? 2:11 talks specifically about the circumcised and uncircumcised, the Jews and the gentiles.

In trying to focus on the concept of "our peace," we must now turn our attention towards this key term in order to understand its meaning. Due to the emotive vocabulary about "peace" in popular evangelicalism (e.g., the hymn "Constantly Abiding"), many will surely see it as a peaceful easy "feeling." This is, in fact, a bad mistake. The peace here has nothing to do with feelings. We can only understand it both in terms of a Jewish background as well as a gentile audience background. Peace often follows grace in all of Paul's greetings. 1:2 is no exception. "Peace" came from the greeting in synagogues "shalom," which signifies relational wholeness in the community with each other as well as with God.

In the imperial context of the audience, Rome promised "the peace of Rome" flowing out from the peace of Augustus, but Paul's gospel promised everlasting peace. The peace of Augustus was an important political theme, especially in places such as Asia Minor. Submission to the emperor will only bring benefit. Why not at least appear to worship him? There is a monument called the "Altar of Peace" that was erected in Athens to show the political importance of Augustus in the East. A similar altar can be seen in a museum in Rome that occupies the entire museum footprint even today.

In this passage, the gospel proclaimed God's plan for peace on earth. The author meant for his Jewish faith to eclipse the promises of the empire. Rome promised the absence of war by using its military machine to suppress all opponents, but the gospel did not need the absence of war to declare peace. Peace was a state of relationship created from friendship among people of vast cultural differences, all because of Christ's rule through the gospel. Peace only follows grace. The one advocating the grace and peace came from God "our Father" instead of the father of the nation, the Roman king. The author declared that God ruled over both Jews and gentiles. Jesus, over against the earthly king, ruled all. Once his audience understood the importance of God's sovereignty through Christ and the gospel, they would be zealous to support the peace between Jews and gentiles. The heart of peace, for the author and for all modern readers, is the sovereignty of God. Besides context, we can also use background information to verify our meaning. We should now see if any background can shed light on the present architectural metaphor.

In order to understand what the author was really talking about, we need to understand the background for the occasion of this letter. By understanding the background, we will once again confirm the meaning we derived from the text. Based on Acts 21:28, Paul was brought to trial because of an accusation against him for bringing gentiles into the Jerusalem temple area. This unrest in Jerusalem finally caused Paul to be imprisoned, which became the occasion for this letter. At least, this is the picture the author of Ephesians presents to us. The accusation had to do with ceremonial problems of gentiles being uncircumcised. The mention of the dividing function of the law is directly related to the original accusation against Paul that came out of the circumstance of his imprisonment. The law (i.e., the Old Testament) here in 2:15 must refer to the very basis of hostility between Jews and gentiles. If Christ abolished the Old Testament function of causing hostility, he then will bring together again the two groups because

*Ephesians 2:14—Which Wall?*

the law distinguished Jews from gentiles. Even though the physical walls of Jerusalem remained standing, Christ's salvation broke that metaphorical wall between Jews and gentiles. The new temple eclipses the old order stipulated by a combination of Jewish and Roman laws. Neither law will bring true salvation to all people. Salvation in Christ, while eliminating the requirements of the old temple, could prepare the audience for their new identity as the new temple in 2:20–21, as passage we shall discuss next. For now, we just have to recognize the temple origin of the architectural image. Here again, the focus is on relationships between different human groups and not between humans and God.

In light of the architectural imagery of this verse, the background of Ephesus is relevant because after all, architecture was ideological. While the city contained one of the largest temples in the ancient world, its Christian community was not primarily defined by a building. It was not defined by the material wealth of the Artemis temple. Rather, the Christian temple was composed of humans. It was a human temple standing in stark contrast against building materials. Its wealth came from the unity between Jewish and gentile believers, a nearly impossible task within the politics of Asia Minor. In seeing this contrast, Paul wrote in order to encourage the believers there to show their superiority by their unity in Christ.

## APPLICATION

The application of this passage is straightforward after the above exegesis. First, we acknowledge that the law is not the problem. Within context, the author was talking about the dividing function of the law between Jews and gentiles. Therefore, the application is not about elimination of the law, even though elsewhere it seems quite clearly and biblically that the function of the law certainly changed after Jesus' death and resurrection. The application should be derived from *how* the author used the content to advance his point rather than *what* the content is. Second, if the law that stood between Jews and gentiles is eliminated to create Christian unity, how much more should other less important differences fall? Thus, Jesus brought peace to reign over all differences between believers. Third, the author was here concerned with ethnic differences. The very fact that churches are completely divided based on ethnicity in any multi-racial and multi-cultural society (e.g., the United States) is problematic. None of this falls within what Jesus originally came for.

The contemporary application is very straightforward. In all societies, buildings are the symbol of prestige and material wealth, sometimes at a cost to the poor. The very same phenomenon happens in Dubai even as I'm writing this. Buildings are the sign of wealth. Such sights and sound create a society obsessed with wealth at all cost. The church needs to respond not by building bigger buildings (necessarily), but by showing its human face through its witness. In such a case, the church can become the benefactor to society, showing the superiority of the gospel to the love of money.

## MISTAKES TO AVOID

The first mistake to avoid is deriving the meaning of a word from preconceived cultural ideas. Even though translation from one language into another (e.g., "peace") can be problematic, context can solve a lot of problems. "Peaceful easy feeling" is part of an Eagles song, not part of this teaching in Ephesians.

The second mistake to avoid is reading only the present content without understanding how the content is used to further the entire argument of the book. By focusing on this verse and that, or this section against another section, the interpreter misses the forest for the trees.

## DISCUSSION QUESTIONS

- What is wrong with the popular sentimental interpretation?
- What did peace mean in the Jewish culture?
- How did the peace of the gospel contrast with the Roman political peace?
- How did the imperial background shed light on the meaning of the verse?
- In what way is the message meaningful for today's church witness?

# 20

# Ephesians 2:20—Prophets Today?

Consequently, you are no longer foreigners and strangers, but fellow citizens with God's people and also members of his household, built on the foundation of the apostles and prophets, with Christ Jesus himself as the chief cornerstone.

## THE POPULAR MEANING

THESE DAYS, THERE ARE a lot of leaders advocating that there are prophets and apostles in the church. Some, such as the Apostolic Movement that started in the early 2000s, cite Ephesians 4:11 as the basis for an end-time five-fold ministry with apostles and prophets at its basis. Some even claim ability to be able to train such prophets and apostles. Somehow, a few in this movement think that the whole solution is to replicate the governing structure of the apostolic age. This passage might have some direct impact towards such claims. To what extent can such claim be verified?

The problem of this passage centers on the phrase "apostles and prophets." The most common interpretation I have heard from sermons is that apostles and prophets represent two parts of God's revelation: the New Testament and the Old. This is from non-charismatics. From the charismatic side, I have heard that this phrase shows that there are clearly New Testament prophets who still hold such offices today. The first interpretation makes a mistake of not taking the order of the pair seriously enough. The second reads today's experience into the text without considering the author's architectural metaphors. Both fall short of the true meaning.

## WHERE DOES THE PASSAGE BEGIN?

There is no need to discuss either structure or background because it has already been covered in our previous chapter.

## THE MEANING OF THE PASSAGE

The foundation in 2:20 must be noted with care. In order for this metaphor to work, some assumptions must be true. First, the order of apostles and prophets fits later with the New Testament gift list in 4:11. People who define prophets as a general term rather than being contextual to the letter are making a serious interpretive mistake here. Moreover, the Greek article (i.e., the equivalent of our English "the") connecting both apostles and prophets shows them to be closely related, though not necessarily speaking of the same group. It stands to reason that if apostles are closely related to prophets, then the time period of the two may be the same. Their ministerial function and authority must also be quite related. "Prophets," then, are the New Testament prophets and not the Old. Otherwise, the order should be "prophets and apostles." What if these are Old Testament prophets? How would they appear in the author's time? In the first century, "prophets" only refers to the Old Testament in the construction "Law and/or Prophets" (e.g., Matthew 5:17).

Second, in order for this metaphor to work, the foundation cannot be rebuilt over and over again. The saying here might have been based on certain construction practices of builders cleaning up ruins and building on top of the former site. At the same time, builders did not repeatedly build a foundation, even if it had been laid a long time ago, unless there was some serious structural problem. Obviously, there can be no addition and no substitution for this foundation. In other words, strictly speaking, the offices of the apostles and prophets as they were practiced in first century no longer exist today, but they did exist while the author was writing. By the plain meaning of the text and all its background, the author already considered them firmly established by the time he wrote Ephesians. He was not looking for more to add to the foundation. This raises the question

## Ephesians 2:20—Prophets Today?

of whether modern day apostles and prophets exist. The answer is a firm negative. In churches today, the ordination of modern-day apostles and prophets in some circles is gravely erroneous.

Having examined the simple problem above, we must use background to interpret the data. The new temple metaphor can teach a lot of lessons when we consider it in its theological, epistolary, and architectural environment. The metaphor here contrasts with the Roman temple and building program in general. Ephesus was the metropolis of Asia. Rome's ambition was to draw everyone together under one empire. The Romans were able to mobilize a lot of people for their building programs, thus communicating imperial power. At the end, they were left with mere corruptible monuments. In contrast, when Christ builds the church, he creates a new humanity, growing upward until he comes. Christ's church far surpasses any building because in Christ, the building remains composed of people and not building materials. Power comes truly from people and not dead buildings. This temple is not a building made of stones—not even expensive stones like Ephesian marble—but an ever growing and ever evolving group of people through the ages. The new temple is not like the temple of Artemis because it is defined by its teachings not by its architecture. Thus, in the first generation of believers, apostles and prophets were building for future generations. Since they had only the Old Testament as a religious foundation, these gifts of apostles and prophets were necessary. The less religious foundation a new movement had, the more likely it would become extinct after the first generation. If someone messed around with the teaching of the apostles and prophets, the church (i.e., the "building") would be in grave danger of becoming extinct. Fortunately, the author had someone like Tychicus who could take care of quality control over the author's teaching when he carried the Ephesian letter (6:21–22).

## APPLICATION

The application of 2:20 and its surrounding context is quite straightforward. It certainly is not about needing prophets for today. Rather, having already had a foundation with apostles and prophets, the church is to grow into a temple against both the social and religious systems of this world. There should be a clear distinction between God's temple and the world's system. The only way to assure quality in this "building" is to gain deep understanding of the teachings of the apostles and prophets. Growth then comes from this deep understanding. A shallow church with shallow teachings will not accomplish this kind of growth. Since the temple represents the God who dwells in it, the church with shallow teaching will fail to represent well.

What can we say about some of the recent emphasis on modern-day apostles and prophets? Nothing! We simply cannot and do not rebuild the foundation of a building. Instead, the church is supposed to build from the first foundation. The passage contains "apostles and prophets" but is not about either one. It is about the church. Today, someone could well claim to have such gifts. Non-charismatics tend to dismiss such claims while charismatics fully buy into such claims. Who is right? We must set limits as to what the passage can do. The passage shows that such gifts exist only alongside the corresponding office and authority. Since there is no office today, can we question whether such associated gifts exist? At the same time, even if (hypothetically) someone has such gift, no such authority should be granted that would attempt to place the gift-holder on par with those in the first century. That is our limit.

The contemporary application is certainly very similar to the other discussion on Ephesians. With humans such as apostles and prophets being the foundation of the church, we can see the contrast once again between the organic nature of the church versus the materialistic nature of societal wealth. However, when the church is in pursuit of wealth and power, her best witness will fall by the wayside.

## MISTAKES TO AVOID

The primary mistake to avoid is simple; do not give theological meaning to biblical terms without first checking the context. Although the wider theological meaning may be helpful, the specific nuance is often missed. The true meaning and application is often in such a nuance. It is a horrible mistake to read letters without historical context. There is a popular strategy of viewing letters mere theological documents. Within them, we certainly derive doctrines but we also need to observe closely their context as actual letters, having specific occasions and specific historical background. Letters are not primarily theological documents. Letters were one-sided conversations between the author and readers. To formulate doctrine from one-sided conversation is less than ideal.

## DISCUSSION QUESTIONS

- What is the problem with either extreme of interpreting "apostles and prophets?"
- What is the author's real message?
- How do we deal with the contemporary issues regarding these offices?
- How are the meanings of this passage limited based on the background and book context?
- What is the best application of the building metaphor for contemporary churches?

# 21

# Ephesians 6:10–18— Putting on the Full Armor of God?

Finally, be strong in the Lord and in his mighty power. Put on the full armor of God, so that you can take your stand against the devil's schemes. For our struggle is not against flesh and blood, but against the rulers, against the authorities, against the powers of this dark world and against the spiritual forces of evil in the heavenly realms. Therefore put on the full armor of God, so that when the day of evil comes, you may be able to stand your ground, and after you have done everything, to stand. Stand firm then, with the belt of truth buckled around your waist, with the breastplate of righteousness in place, and with your feet fitted with the readiness that comes from the gospel of peace. In addition to all this, take up the shield of faith, with which you can extinguish all the flaming arrows of the evil one. Take the helmet of salvation and the sword of the Spirit, which is the word of God.

And pray in the Spirit on all occasions with all kinds of prayers and requests. With this in mind, be alert and always keep on praying for all the Lord's people.

## THE POPULAR MEANING

ENTIRE INDUSTRIES HAVE BEEN built around interpretation of and (mostly) speculations about this passage. There are warfare prayers, warfare books, and warfare movies propagated out there. Books on spiritual warfare have been the main diet of many popular readers' consumption.

*Ephesians 6:10–18—Putting on the Full Armor of God?*

The fact of the matter is, this entire passage has been so twisted into anything and everything that its original meaning is hardly detectable in most of such popular books. Books have borrowed language from this passage to talk about something quite different than the precise meaning of the author. The distortion of the message of Ephesians 6 is like the modern distortion of Christmas being primarily about Santa Claus. Neither represents the true message.

What can be made of this passage? Scholars of the past, especially those with non-evangelical convictions, have debated endlessly the definition of "principalities and powers." "In the heavenly places" seems to be a clear enough phrase to put beyond doubt that the author was talking about demonic forces, which goes against many of the anti-supernatural interpretations of many Western interpreters. Whether modern interpreters agree with the biblical author or not, all those in the biblical world took it for granted that such forces exist, without dwelling much on them. The author of Ephesians assumed his audience had an understanding of such forces as well, not unlike many corners of the third-world today. Most likely, the debate here can generate two strands of thoughts: supernatural and political interpretations. I'm not convinced that the author did not see supernatural within the political realm of Ephesus. The division may be more of a modern construct rather than a reflection of the author's ancient worldview. We must move on to more important issues.

The most common understanding of this passage among lay people and academics alike is that each Christian should put on his armor and fight the devil. We shall see below that this is an absolutely incorrect application, not only because it is too individualistic, but because it is also grammatically unsustainable.

## WHERE DOES THE PASSAGE BEGIN?

Naturally, this passage is part of the wider context of Ephesians. Exactly how should we divide it? Ephesians 6:10 starts with a command. The Greek form shows a clear mood of command. The verse starts with "finally," which signifies that the passage has a final topic with an imperative as its main verb. Prior to this, the author had a series of commands that led up to this "finally." Thus, it is important to deal with 6:10 as part of an orderly series of commands. Thus, the order of all the commands is intentional, starting with commands for the whole church in 5:15–21, leading to commands for the family in 5:22—6:9, and then climaxing at 6:10, again for the whole church.

## THE MEANING OF THE PASSAGE

Beyond metaphysical debates about the supernatural, I think the trickier part is the obvious application of this passage (that is not obvious at all for the average interpreter). The passage is harder to apply than it looks because most apply it individually. Indeed, the Stoics in ancient times used the warfare metaphor for individuals. If we apply it individually only, we are more like the Stoics than Christians. The image here was quite different from the Stoics'. The author's application mostly has to do with the church's corporate direction. The language he used is very specific and nuanced. The reason I say this is because of the presence of the second person plural "you" in several places in this passage and first person plural "our" in 6:12 with the singular "armor." How do all these people put on *one* armor? They should put on many sets of armors, one for each soldier. Yet, that is not what the text says.

The mixture of singular armor with the plurals is indeed confusing, and if this fact was shared from the pulpit, many modern Christians would become extremely confused. But if it is not shared, the result is even more dire. Thus, the author's application points the way for the church's direction. The armor metaphor fits well since the New Testament often pictures the church as the "body." So, this passage is *not* mainly about individuals putting on armor. In fact, the individualistic model is in contradiction to the spirit of this passage. The individual is not meant to fight against the devil. The church is! Better yet, the passage points towards church leaders, who should take responsibility to make sure their church culture possess the godly qualities listed.

This corporate model fits perfectly with the context of the household code on the responsibilities of the husbands, fathers, and masters. All those with responsibilities also happened to be the early house church leaders, because that was the way society worked in that time. The author's corporate command makes sense because of the connection between house churches and the individual family members. It also makes sense in terms of how the entire Roman Empire was viewed as one big household under the leadership of the emperor. Now since the Roman "household" was not merely a nuclear family (like our modern conception of "family") but was a complex network including slaves and extended families, the author expected the change in Christian life not to occur just on the individual's lives but in the way the Greco-Roman leaders ran their household networks. The series of commands was meant to be applied corporately. The Christian

*Ephesians 6:10–18—Putting on the Full Armor of God?*

household should be outshining the secular political household (i.e., the Empire). The subsequent commands have five components.

First, in 6:10, "be strong" can be translated to "be strengthened" as the command is in the Greek passive form. God, and not the individual believer or even the church, then, becomes the strengthening force. The church becomes the entity that submits under God's rule. Second, the next command is to put on the full armor of God in 6:11, 13. The Greek of the command in 6:11 also conveys a sense of necessity, corporate responsibility, and urgency. Third, the church must stand firm in 6:14. Clearly the evil one is trying to cause the church to fall. Fourth, the church is to take on salvation and God's word in 6:17. Fifth, the church must pray in 6:18–20.

We should also look now at 6:10–20 as a part of the long ending starting at 5:15. If 6:10 represents the climax, then the family passage is about preparation for the climax. In other words, if the family problem was not solved, corporate spiritual victory could be realized. Thus, the unity extends from the family to the church. Why is this? It is because the ancient churches met in homes. If the household did not witness to all visitors, then the church would have no impact on the world. In other words, the way the household deals within the society ought to become the great example and witness. Then comes victory.

## APPLICATION

After looking at the passage in terms of corporate application, what must be understood in the metaphor of the armor? Much of the armor list can be applied either in our interpersonal relationships or our relationship to God. The only offensive weapon is the word of God. Without recognizing the unity and relational aspects, the church will lose no matter what kind of magical rituals or prayers certain Christian gurus are proposing these days. This is a great point of summary of the teachings in 2:15 and 4:22–24. The church is the new man. The metaphor of warfare shows the church's existence on this earth as having suffering and difficulty, not health, wealth, and prosperity. Life on earth is not supposed to be easy. The limited and veiled descriptions for the evil forces use political vocabulary, showing the enemy as an organized force. In the first century, it may be have been organized through the social-political system or the occult. In other words, victory is something that happens in the ordinary and not something superstitious or mystical. The embodiment of Christ in the unity of the church wins the war. How can that embodiment happen?

Let me first state what it is not. Many Christians think that the cultural war against secularism is the answer to spiritual war. They could not be more wrong! First-century society was thoroughly secular and pluralistic, but the author didn't focus on attacking the society. Many Christians expect unbelievers to act like believers. They decry this or that moral shortfall. The entire cultural war effort between the religious right and the secular left is wrong-headed and does not fit the message here.

The whole discussion of the network of relationships within the Roman household helps a great deal when applying this text to modern life. Many Christians only act like Christians when they are in church. The Christian lifestyle needs to penetrate to the way we operate in our business, school, and family lives. Our complex networks should recognize that Christians are a changed people. If our relationships have not changed and our ethics have not become better, the battle is decisively lost. Faith is public, and the battle is relational.

The church together also needs to benefit society through the networks of her membership. Evangelism, for example, should not come in the form of modern evangelistic crusade methods. Rather, evangelism should happen naturally through daily lives and relationships. That's how embodiment happens. That's how the battle is won.

## MISTAKES TO AVOID

The first mistake to avoid is the lack of awareness of the author's usage of plural pronouns. He used so many plural pronouns that are too often applied only to individuals rather than the entire church. This is a simple, but terrible, intepretive mistake that narrows the impact of the gospel.

The second mistake is not seeing where the passage fits within the letter. As we noticed, this passage fits the letter very well as a climax of a series of orderly and logical commands for Christian, and indeed churchly, living.

## DISCUSSION QUESTIONS

- What is wrong with the popular interpretations of spiritual warfare?
- What does the mixture of plurals and singulars in such a passage indicate?
- What is the message of this passage in terms of its surrounding context?
- How does this teaching apply to churches, families, and individuals today?

# 22

# Philippians 2:5— Same Attitude as Christ's?

In your relationships with one another, have the same mindset as Christ Jesus....

## THE POPULAR MEANING

ONCE AGAIN, LIKE SO many popular interpretations of this study, many have taken Philippians 2:5 to be a general statement so that we can have the attitude of Jesus. Bloggers have a field day with this verse. One delves into what a human mind is like and then begins matching what God's mind is like. Perhaps, she should offer a course on the psychology of God! Another simply interprets the verse to mean that we ought to think what God thinks. Who knows what God is thinking anyway? Still another blends in all kinds of verses related to the mind in the New Testament, trying to explain this concept of the mind of Christ. The list of such variations is as numerous as the number of popular interpreters. From our discussion below, we shall see that the popular interpretations are once again lacking. Paul did not mean for this verse to turn into a general statement, but meant something quite specific, when applying it to a Christian's life.

## WHERE DOES THE PASSAGE BEGIN?

The translations have the passage beginning in 2:1 where it starts with "therefore." While "therefore" shows a new sentence and paragraph, it also connects the present with the previous context. Perhaps the last truly independent clause we can find is in 1:27. I think this is a good assessment of where 2:1 comes from. We may use 1:27 as the starting point to gauge our meaning. Another reason for using 1:27 as the beginning of this unit of thought is because it is where Paul makes the transition from narrating about his situation to exhorting the Philippians. The exhortation continues right through the verses we are trying to study.

## THE MEANING OF THE PASSAGE

Philippians, for all its pleasantries, is hard to categorize. Many scholars have agreed to see it as a friendship letter. With its mostly pleasant and encouraging tone, Paul gave a sense that he was concerned both for the persecution coming from the outside and the conflict coming from the inside (e.g., 1:28; 3:2; 4:2–3). It is therefore, important to keep these challenges in mind. Paul wrote 2:5 in light of such challenges.

2:5 is key to understanding a lot of what follows because it is the beginning sentence to which verses 2:6–11 serve as modifying clauses. Thus, the meaning of 2:5 is incomplete because 2:6–11 defines the meaning for it, and not apart from it. There are many ways to interpret the Christ hymn afterwards, but the important thing is to find a certain amount of consensus so that we can get a handle on the material to interpret 2:5.

The part that follows 2:5 is categorized by many scholars to be a hymn of some kind, even though others prefer to see another genre in it. The section ought to be divided into two parts. 2:6–8 is one part and 2:9–11 is another. 2:2 starts with what would really please Paul: a sense of unity in attitude and ideal. The first phrase of 2:2 talks about being like-minded which essentially means "thinking the same thing." The second phrase of 2:2 talks about possessing love. Paul further expressed the kind of love he meant by calling it "being of same spirit." With the intensity of Paul's compound sentence, in which he piled one idea upon another, we get the sense that he was intensely concerned with a certain oneness that is essential to body life. By illustrating what does not contribute to Paul's idea of oneness, 2:3–4 gives a series of strong antitheses, leading up to 2:5. Philippians 2:5 defines the basis for that oneness. In other words, 2:5 further clarifies the meaning of 2:2–4.

## Philippians 2:5—Same Attitude as Christ's?

What then is the meaning of 2:5? 2:6–8 talks about what Christ did. He did three things: he didn't regard equality with God as something to be grasped; he emptied himself (though Paul didn't say emptying himself of what); and he humbled himself by being obedient. The very center of this discussion is the cross. Paul here talked about Christ from his pre-incarnate state to his crucifixion. Where exactly Paul got this hymn, no one knows. It is possible that he composed it. It is also possible, as many scholars have claimed, that Paul borrowed it from early church tradition. Scholars also cannot agree on the meaning of this hymn.

For the most part, scholars do not think it is implied that Christ emptied his divinity. The divine nature of Christ was only much more clearly stated after later church councils (though we can be sure there have been hints all through the New Testament of this divinity). One thing is sure: Paul asserted that Christ emptied himself by ironically taking on the form of a slave. There may be a hint of what Christ had emptied himself of in 2:3 where the word "empty" is also linked with empty glory. Perhaps Paul was using a roundabout way of saying that Christ had allowed his glory to be veiled by the servile form. Whatever the precise meaning, Christ voluntarily moved from the highest height of heavenly position to the pit of human existence. Yet, all is not gloom and doom.

Paul then turned to the second part of the hymn, depicting the award of Jesus' obedience in 2:9–11. This is no doubt where the gloom turns into glory because the sentence starts with "therefore" in 2:9. The results of exaltation are easily found in 2:10–11. Jesus would be exalted to the highest place. Then, everyone would confess that Jesus is Lord. These words are greatly theological but also quite sociological. In that time, only masters or Caesar were called "Lord." Yet, Jesus became the Lord of all. This metaphor must have meant a lot to the audience because they lived in a Roman colony. They would be greatly encouraged.

What then does 2:5 mean in light of all the discussions so far? First, it would mean that those who were able to humble themselves would be able to put aside personal differences with their fellow believers (cf. 4:2). True Lordship of Jesus produces unity and humility.

## APPLICATION

Humility is hard to come by. It is easy to generalize about imitating Jesus and having the same mind as Jesus, and so on. The Christian church is full of spiritualized language. Yet, when it comes down to conflicts, no one is willing to back down. Paul's command is not for us to go through a little feel-good exercise about being like Christ in a general sense. Rather, he was telling the audience to be humble like Jesus, so much so that he had sacrificed himself in service to humanity, even serving unto death. Thus, the heart of Christ Paul was talking about was humility. The expression of this heart is sacrificial service.

It is quite common that churches these days are filled with those who are quick to voice their opinions but are not quite as quick to serve. Paul's admonition to his audience has much to say to our increasingly divided Christianity. Quite often, people divide and unite for all the wrong reasons. From the lesson of Philippians, we must notice that division over trivial matters is not helpful to the unity of the church. At the same time, unity in spite of heresies and falsehood is also equally harmful. Paul did not hesitate to point to the Christ hymn as his theological and ethical standard. This usage surely informs us about what to divide and unite over.

## MISTAKES TO AVOID

The first mistake, like so many passages, is the generalization of a particular passage into some life principle with no understanding of what is said before or after. Christ's heart here can create serious problems for people who do not know what it actually means in light of context.

The second mistake is to ignore the wider book context. We can see from the wider book context that the Philippian church had experienced incredible challenges, both external and internal. By keeping the wider book context in mind, a critical verse like 2:5 comes alive for application.

## DISCUSSION QUESTIONS

- What is wrong with the many popular interpretations of this verse?
- What concerned Paul in this passage?
- How would unity and having the mind of Christ be related?
- How might Paul's concern be reflected in our modern churches?

# 23

# 1 Timothy 4:8—
# An Excuse *Not* to Keep Fit?

For physical training is of some value, but godliness has value for all things, holding promise for both the present life and the life to come.

### THE POPULAR MEANING

EXERCISING IS NOT HIGH on some people's to-do lists. One joke goes, "If God wanted me to touch my toes, he would've made them higher." I happen to be one of those who love exercising. Knowing how much I value physical training and fitness, this verse, more than any other verse, has been used to "encourage" me not to keep so fit, quite often by "spiritual" people, even pastors, who could use a whole lot of exercise themselves. Trouble is, if people do not know the proper historical context and word meanings of such a verse, they can easily see this as some kind of dualistic view of the human, favoring a certain "spiritual" aspect over the "physical" aspect. Nothing is further from the truth.

### WHERE DOES THE PASSAGE BEGIN?

The passage most likely starts its unit of thought in 4:1, where the author now gave advice to Timothy the church leader. The entire letter deals with both external and internal challenges to the church. While the previous chapter talks about the internal structure of the church, this chapter talks about external danger. Timothy not only needed to know such danger, but also needed to point it out to his congregation (4:6).

## THE MEANING OF THE PASSAGE

We have already stated, the letter dealt with external and internal challenges facing Timothy. The mistake most people make is to apply this verse to the church's internal "physical" realm. Let me suggest that we look closely at the context and see that the church and Timothy were facing external pressure. The letter was the advice to Timothy on how to cope.

The context of the letter seems quite straightforward. There are various theories as to what the heresy actually was. We do not need to go into theories at this point because no one can be certain. The text tells us the following characteristics of this heretical teaching: prohibition of marriage (4:3) and abstinence from certain food (4:3).

In light of the external pressure from potential heresy, the author gave important advice in 4:6-8. The author first told Timothy to uphold good teaching in 4:6. He then told Timothy to shun godless teachings in 4:7. Then comes the key verse in question in 4:8. We must start by observing that 4:8 starts with a "for" which means the author was giving a reason why Timothy had to train to become godly. It seems on the surface to point to Timothy's own spirituality, unless we read it in the context of 4:6-7. This is when knowing the meaning of Greek words is helpful.

4:8 talks about "physical training." The Greek word for "physical training" results in the English word for "gymnasium" but is not exactly the same meaning as the English. This kind training was part of the ancient schoolboy's training. It was like our gym class today in school but had more elements. The Greeks were not only concerned with mental and intellectual fitness, but were also concerned with physical fitness. Our physical education for youth usually has one component, the exercise part. The ancient Greek physical training had two separate components. First, as it is commonly understood today, this training involved sports and exercise. Second, as it is less commonly known and infrequently practiced today, this training involved an athlete's diet. The diet in turn would bring fitness to the trainee. In this way, the Greeks were more holistic in their approach than modern physical education!

*1 Timothy 4:8—An Excuse Not to Keep Fit?*

The second part of physical training was especially important for understanding the context. In 4:3, the false teaching clearly related to diet. This prior context sets the meaning for 4:8. In other words, the author was advocating for Timothy not to be pressured by heretical teachings or certain ascetic tendencies within his congregation to go on a certain diet. 5:23 once again discussed diet with a focus on allowing wine drinking. This, then, verifies that certain dietary asceticism was beginning to pressure Timothy, quite possibly from heretical teachings coming from the outside. The meaning here, in light of the context, surely suggests precise applications, as we shall see below.

## APPLICATION

The admonition to Timothy is applicable today, not in terms of fitness, but in terms of several other areas. Timothy seems to be facing undue pressure that is not merely inhibiting his Christian freedom, but also giving a false image of what the gospel is. More specific is the appearance of piety through asceticism. In today's church, there are some self-imposed ascetics who advocate this or that spiritual discipline (which is fine in and of itself). But then they also begin defining spirituality based on such appearances and try to force others to walk their path. The author sensed this kind of challenge and he wanted Timothy not to give in.

We must take note that New Testament discussions elsewhere urge serious caution about such controversial matter as food law, but only in the context of causing a truly weak believer to stumble. Here, there was no such danger. Rather, the appearance of Timothy might have caused others to have the wrong idea of what the gospel was all about. Perhaps, Timothy was doing this to keep peace in the church. Peace came at a heavy cost. In such a case, the author advocated that Timothy should take all his Christian liberties, and not be controlled by unnecessary pressure. It is the exact opposite of asceticism and physical neglect (including, possibly, refraining from exercising and extreme forms of fasting).

Since the heresy here seems to come from Timothy's surrounding culture, there is yet another application. When contextualizing the gospel, there is also a danger of compromising with the culture. Many do so in the name of the gospel, thus creating an impression that the gospel and culture completely blend. The author also wanted to show that the gospel was radical and different from culture. How can we separate the two? The more we understand the central truth of the gospel (which seems to concern the author here), the more we can separate the two.

## MISTAKES TO AVOID

The first mistake to avoid is the lack of understanding of historical background. Many read the Pastorals like some kind of ministry handbook. This is wrong. It is the same essential mistake people commit with the letters when they dogmatize the teaching without attention to their historical background.

The second mistake to avoid is the lack of understanding of literary context and authorial purpose. When all else fails, meanings should come from the literary context, verified by the broader context of the letter. When this is left undone, we hear applications such as, "Paul does not care about the body," which are certainly refuted soundly in other texts, such as 1 Corinthians 15.

The third mistake to avoid is the lack of understanding of word meanings. Even if we know Greek, modern assumptions about word meanings can skew our interpretations. In this case, a more careful word study would benefit interpretation of this verse and many other words, because words have ranges of meanings based on backgrounds.

## DISCUSSION QUESTIONS

- What is wrong with the popular interpretation?
- How does the verse relate to the letter's context?
- How can this verse apply in today's world?

# 24

## 2 Timothy 3:16—
## "All" Scripture Is "God-Breathed?"

All Scripture is God-breathed and is useful for teaching, rebuking, correcting and training in righteousness....

### THE POPULAR MEANING

THIS VERSE IS ESPECIALLY abused by beginning systematic theology students who use it to "prove" that Scripture is without error. Some evangelicals have even used it as the litmus test and cornerstone of orthodoxy, quite often without knowing the meaning of the verse. After reading the discussion below, we shall see that any doctrinal debate should be by implication rather than from "proof text."

### WHERE DOES THE PASSAGE BEGIN?

The passage best starts in 3:10 where the author contrasted Timothy with the godless heretics described in 3:1–9. The sentence begun in 3:16 ends at 3:17.

### THE MEANING OF THE PASSAGE

In 3:10–13, the author (likely Paul) set himself up as an ethical model by narrating to Timothy what he already knew. This model is exhortative to

Timothy because 3:10 starts with an emphatic "you, however" which separates Timothy from the godlessness of 3:1–9. The author's encouragement included the recounting of how God had delivered him from various persecutions (3:11b). The author suggested that hard times would come for Timothy and had indeed come for himself. Timothy would also face hard times while his agitators would once again get away with heresies (3:12–13), but out of God's mercy, he will receive deliverance. Quite often, people quote 3:12 as a general statement about everyone who has lived a godly life, but I believe Paul was referring specifically to conditions in his own time. Even in the New Testament, not all godly people in every age faced persecution.

This brings us to a good dividing point in our main text starting in 3:14. The reason I say that it's a good dividing point is because it starts with an emphatic singular "you" just like the emphatic "you" in 3:10, that indicated a dividing point from 3:1–9. The key command is the verb "continue," or as I prefer to translate it, "remain" in 3:14. Timothy was doing something right, and Paul wanted to encourage him to remain in his vocation. What exactly was Timothy doing right? The author clearly indicated that Timothy had been educated since his youth about the Scriptures by sound teachers. Here I'm assuming the sound teachers to include Paul, Paul's coworkers, and possible Timothy's grandmother Lois and his mother Eunice (1:5). If these women were not completely literate, as was commonly the case for women, then perhaps those who taught the women were also responsible for teaching Timothy. More importantly, the author most likely contributed as well (1:6).

It is worth pondering how long Timothy had known the Scriptures, based on our educated guesses. If Lois was his grandmother, we must guess that Lois and Eunice were first generation believers who had probably heard sermons from Diaspora missionaries about Jesus the Christ, perhaps from the returnees of Pentecost. Christianity (or more accurately "messianic Judaism"), as Timothy knew it (especially after Paul's conversion) had only existed for a little more than three decades. This puts Timothy's knowledge base strictly in the Old Testament because none of the New Testament books had yet been written. Or if any parts of the New Testament were written, the writings were not yet considered Scripture until later (cf. 2 Peter 3:15–16). Therefore, this timeline is sufficient to explain 3:16, where "all Scripture" actually means very clearly the Old Testament, not the New Testament. In this passage, the author used two different but related words to describe Scriptures. In 3:15, he used a word that focuses on the written letter in contrast to the musings of the heretics in the passage before. In 3:16, he used a word that describes Scripture in its entirety. In other words, the author wanted to stress the concrete written words on the one hand and the wholly inspired nature on the other. What is the nature of the Old Testament then?

According to the author, it is "God-breathed." The word is hard to translate. The reason why translators have trouble translating is because the author created this word. The form in the Greek is passive indicating that God was doing the work and the Scripture was receiving it. Thus, the Old Testament is no doubt the work of God. This word does not, in contradistinction to some evangelical's conviction, speak of the mode of inspiration (whether dictation by God or otherwise), but only that it is the work of God. What functions does the Old Testament have, though?

The Old Testament, according to the author, is good for teaching, rebuking, correcting, and training in righteousness. Teaching is for those who are ignorant and need to be taught. Rebuking is for those who have done terribly wrong. Correcting is for setting the wrong on the right path. Training in righteousness is for those who need the discipline to stay on the straight and narrow. The purpose of this teaching ministry is quite clear as stated in 3:17. The author saw the Old Testament as the way to equip people to do good work for God.

What can we sum up from the entirety of the context of this verse? In keeping with authorial purpose and concern, the text does not only talk about the formation and nature of the Old Testament, but it shows the importance of its role in fighting heresies. The author recognized that he was about to depart. The legacy he would leave was not the transfer of personal authority but the apostolic succession of teaching ministry based on the Old Testament, the only Scripture Timothy had.

## APPLICATION

This verse is highly applicable. It shows the high bar of leadership the author expected of his coworkers, who would carry on his legacy. Let us compare with today's leadership and expectations. We have fallen to a much lower level. When we listen to our pulpit preaching, we can hardly find any preaching on the Old Testament (or more properly called, Hebrew Bible) any more. In the US, a favorable and popular style has to be entertaining. There is rarely exegesis of Scripture that does any of the things the author said the Scripture should do. Even those who quote 2 Timothy 3:16 to further the most conservative model of biblical inspiration fail miserably when it comes to preaching a balance of the Old and New Testaments. Some seminaries have made biblical languages optional in favor of more "practical and creative" programs. Other seminaries have done slightly better by only requiring one biblical language. Still others have lightened up the load on all biblical exegesis courses while keeping the same credit hours. This goes to show how far removed our present situation is from the spirit of this verse.

We must further notice that the author did not focus on the personality of the leader too much, but focused on the teaching, and the bequeathing of the teaching to the next generation. As Christians, the verse teaches us to go back to our Old Testament roots and understand the meaning of many of its difficult passages. That would be the plain sense application of the verses here.

## MISTAKES TO AVOID

The first mistake to avoid is reading a meaning into the text without proper checking of context. In this case, divorced from context the verse can be used to prove any and everything. As we can see from the above, its meaning is actually quite limited and specific. It was not meant to prove anything. Instead, the verse is there to encourage Timothy to carry on his duty. It teaches the usefulness of the Old Testament, and that no one should neglect its teaching and still expect to equip the person of God for every good work.

The second mistake to avoid is the lack of appreciation for the polemical context of the passage prior to this verse. The author clearly showed in 3:1–9 the importance of the Old Testament in fighting heresies. Quite often, this context is neglected in favor of reading the verse as a doctrinal statement. This should not be. The rhetoric of this entire passage shows that the best defense against heresies is not merely to research the heresies. Instead, teaching the Bible faithfully will eliminate heresies in the church.

## DISCUSSION QUESTIONS

- What is wrong with the popular understanding of this verse?
- What is the main focus of this verse?
- What meanings are impossible for this verse?
- How does taking a verse like this seriously impact the teaching ministry of the church?

# 25

# James 3:1–2—
# Watching Your Tongue?

> Not many of you should become teachers, my fellow believers, because you know that we who teach will be judged more strictly. We all stumble in many ways. Anyone who is never at fault in what they say is perfect, able to keep their whole body in check.

## THE POPULAR MEANING

WHEN WE WERE YOUNG, we often had to face the challenge of tongue twisters. The fun thing about tongue twisters is that we can say something entirely unintended, if we are not careful. Such is the power and weakness of the tongue. James 3:2–12 has always been considered a section on moral teaching about the tongue. So, every believer should try to control the tongue. The passage seems straightforward enough. However, my observation about interpretations is, if a passage seems too straightforward, it is usually because we have not considered its context well enough, either in historical background or within the surrounding texts.

Many people consider James to be easy and full of maxims. Its deceptive easiness is precisely where the difficulty lies, because by fragmenting one topic from another, James's writing begins to look like a stream of consciousness style that rambles endlessly. James, however, is highly logical and his Greek is fairly sophisticated. With such a learned disposition, would a man such as James just randomly comment on this or that idea? Likely not.

## WHERE DOES THE PASSAGE BEGIN?

The passage begins, simply enough at James 3:1. It is a continuation of the topic of faith having some lively deeds to back it up. Many people read 3:1 without considering 3:2–12. Although 3:2 starts a new sentence, it is a continuation of the thought coming out of James 3:1.

## THE MEANING OF THE PASSAGE

The meaning of the passage must be governed by 3:1 because 3:1 grounds the entire passage in a concrete background. It seems that there were people in James's community who wanted to become teachers and James was trying to warn them.

First, James started with a warning that those who would speak loosely because they would face judgment. What qualified one to teach in a synagogue? At the very least, literacy was the basic qualification. The Jews had a higher literacy rate simply because of their focus on sacred Scripture. Now, in order to achieve the literacy level of a teacher (like Paul or James), people probably had to have some resources and time. Jesus was able to teach his disciples because there were plenty of financial sponsors who were willing to help out (e.g., Luke 8:1–3). Those who were teachers might have come from the upper financial class of the community. In order to become a synagogue teacher, the Jewish man had to go through vigorous training as part of a selected group of boys during their pre-teen years in order to qualify. Having rhetorical skill was the sign of high social class. Literacy was not enough. The ability to think well also came into play. These and other skills were necessary steps of becoming a teacher in those days. James however did not focus on skills, because skills were prerequisites.

It seems that somehow James himself had acquired a decent education that had impacted his writing of the Greek language and leadership in the church. In Acts 15:13–21, he was one of the ruling leaders of the church as they considered the issue of circumcision. In his ruling in the apostolic council, James clearly demonstrated a deep knowledge of Scripture when he persuaded those around him that his point of view was right. In Paul's letters to the Galatians (Galatians 1–2), James played an important role.

The fact that James was not one of the twelve apostles but had such a high role of leadership speaks well of his knowledge. Thus, besides his sophisticated Greek, circumstantial evidence demands that we see James as a well-educated leader who would certainly know about the educational system that helped many rhetorically strong people succeed. Of all the people in the early church, he was among the most qualified leaders to address the problem of skills without character.

Second, James admonished all those who taught to have control over their speech in 3:2. To James, the mark of self-control was pure speech. James then followed his train of thought to discuss the importance of having control of the tongue (3:2–12). Quite frequently, commentators and popular preachers look at this section and immediately assume that this is talking only about the Christian usage of the tongue. In reality, this is just a continuation of James's discussion about qualifications to teach. In order to understand the fullness of what James was talking about and the problem James was dealing with, we should also look at the wider context in James.

It is absolutely vital to notice that judgment vocabulary also occurs in 2:12–13. There, the judgment is against those who were unmerciful to the poor. James further discussed and dismissed claims (presumably verbal claims) of faith without deeds as being a false faith, in 2:14, 18. And in fact, the whole tongue issue goes all the way back to 1:26. In other words, James was dealing with the same problems and possibly the same group of people all along. If we were to describe this group of folks James was denouncing, we can say that they were socially selfish and uncompassionate towards the oppressed, while striving to be leaders by being teachers. James then was dealing not so much with skills issues, but rather character issues.

This passage in James 3 shows that the teachers had a lot of power in the congregation and many were striving towards that power. Some were arguing one way while acting a different way. Some were speaking half-truths. With all this in mind, the present passage ought to address those who strived for higher leadership in the church. Their skill sets and doctrines were important (James assumed them in 2:14–26), but their character was more important (James assumed it in 2:26—3:12). Instead of using their mouths to get ahead, they ought to use their resources to help the poor.

## APPLICATION

This passage, in light of what was said above, is not mainly applying towards the tongue, though it does implicate the ordinary usage of the tongue. Control over the tongue is vital in spiritual health. The passage applies more, however, in the area of church leadership. Skills are not enough, even though they are necessary. The main issue was not the tongue but the skills involved in powerful positions. These days, people aim for skills more than ever. In James's day, skills were trained up and learned. Thus, we should value training and skills. More importantly, we should add something extra to skills. We should be strong on character.

The above discussion should not necessarily apply to teachers and pastoral candidates only because teaching might not be the only way to get ahead in church leadership these days. Whatever higher position Christians strive for in serving God, James's advice would be for the believer to work his character and good works. In other words, James expected a real demonstration of faith before anyone could take up leadership positions in churches.

## MISTAKES TO AVOID

This passage is easily narrowed down to some convoluted and overly simplistic applications for today. The mistake is the isolation of 3:2–12 without doing any study on the surrounding passages, because everything around the passage defines its meaning.

The chapter division has once again wreaked havoc on popular interpretation. A little word study on words like "judge" in 3:1 (and 2:12–13) and "tongue" in 3:2 (and 1:26–27) will yield some different interpretive results. The meaning is all right there, if we bother to notice the words James used.

## DISCUSSION QUESTIONS

- What is not exactly right about the popular meaning?
- What was the greater concern for James besides the tongue?
- What are the implications about the kind of people who should lead?
- What is the message for us today?

# PART THREE

Popularly Misused Texts
in Apocalyptic Literature

# 26

## Revelation 3:16, 20—
## Lukewarm? An Invitation to Unbelievers?

"So, because you are lukewarm—neither hot nor cold—I am about to spit you out of my mouth....

"Here I am! I stand at the door and knock. If anyone hears my voice and opens the door, I will come in and eat with that person, and they with me."

### THE POPULAR MEANING

ONE FAMOUS PASTOR'S FACEBOOK update reads, "Nowhere does the Bible say, 'Because you are white hot, I will spew you out of my mouth.'" Revelation 3:16 normally has a popular interpretation that there are many warm Christians who are neither cold nor hot. The discussion then centers on spiritual temperature. We will see that such a formulation is not right.

Revelation 3:20 has been used in quite a few evangelistic tools. The message usually goes something like this: Jesus is outside the door of our hearts. We must open our hearts to him and he'll come in to dine with us and we with him. We will see that this is definitely a wrong interpretation of the verse.

We'll discuss these verses together simply because they are within the same context. There is no need to keep them separated while we analyze the same context.

## WHERE DOES THE PASSAGE BEGIN?

The passage is part of an ongoing letter to the church of Laodicea. The passage begins in 3:14 and ends at 3:22. It is the last of the seven "letters" written to the churches.

## Excursus: A Very Brief Introduction to Apocalyptic Literature

I was born in Hong Kong and immigrated to the US when I was young. Thus, I am completely bilingual. Just because I am bilingual, however, does not mean that I am completely attuned to the cultural and linguistic changes in Hong Kong and China. The first time I returned was for professional reasons. Since then, I have had chances to lecture and teach there. I recall once sharing a platform with one of the region's most famous scholars of preaching and New Testament. We were discussing the topic of contemporary preaching with our audience. He showed a film clip of a recent TV comedy. While the entire audience was laughing, I had no idea why the comedy was funny. I understood all the words, but I hardly found humor or meaning in the dialogue. The cultural differences between me and the audience were just too great. I understood the words, but I did not understand the connotations behind the words. Sometimes, when we read apocalyptic literature, the very same thing happens. Our culture does not have apocalyptic literature.

Before we understand anything about any part of Revelation, we must discuss what exactly apocalyptic literature is. The brief introduction here will be enough for what we are trying to accomplish with our subsequent discussions on Revelation.

First, John wrote that this is not *the* revelation but *a* revelation among many within the New Testament (1:1). In so doing, John recognizes that there is a wider community of Christian writers and he is accountable to them, but sees his own contribution to be significant. The word "revelation" means to unveil but it does not tell us much of anything. The revelation itself is uniquely different from the surrounding religions in that it was neither the pagan mystery, nor religious formalities, nor traditional myths, nor political ideologies, but an eternal plan of God in ages past which is now unveiled for all to see.

The book is also unique from any literature of our day simply because there is not any such genre today (with the possible exception of some science fiction novels). The world the book describes is otherworldly. Although we have no such genre today, in John's day and the periods before, people utilized the genre often as a tool for political commentary. Their otherworldly language might cause modern readers to think that the genre was all about otherworldly situations, but the otherworldly language was meant to describe the author's situation, coded in symbolic language. Authors often used symbols they could see in their world to convey their own view towards politics, society, and God. To put matters simply, although we may not understand all the figures, the readers of Revelation would have already understood the genres, figures, and meanings of the book. In this sense, Revelation is no different from other books of the New Testament. All biblical literature can only be understood fully when read according to the genre, the text, and the cultural and historical contexts.

To all sensible Bible readers, it should be no surprise that Scripture is not a crystal ball. In Christian belief, the text is first and foremost God's revelation to humanity through human authors within human history. As such, the Bible is revealed first through the ancient writers to the ancient audience. By understanding both, we the modern believer can find the implications and form our applications, if we so desire. Revelation is often treated differently as some kind of especially supernatural document, as if it is some kind of mythological tale encoding modern events. It is not! Instead, it is the narration of a series of visions.

John's stated purpose in the prologue was to exhort listeners to take the message seriously and to live accordingly (1:3) because he sure is doing that. "Take to heart" is not some kind of intellectual exercise, but is knowledge accompanied by action. According to 1:9b, John is either confined to Patmos or the Lord has instructed him to go to Patmos to receive visions. More than likely, he was confined due to the fact that he had to send a letter to the seven churches because he could not be there personally to present the message.

The book plainly speaks about writing to an original audience of the seven churches. The seven churches that were on the Roman roads became hubs of all the messages that God wants to let "him who has ears" hear (2:7, 11, 17, 29; 3:6, 13, 22). More than likely, Asia Minor churches eventually got to listen to this book being read to them. Most of the book contains series of visions. Revelation is a "vision" that must be seen through the Greco-Roman audience's world, not merely words to be studied or text to be microscopically analyzed without context. All understanding should be gained through an attempt to understand their world and vision.

In final summary, Revelation is an ethical book that contains the best mixture of ancient epistolary, prophetic, and apocalyptic literatures. By keeping it firmly within its time and social background, I begin to "see" a timeless vision. After looking closely at what the visions meant, the meaning emerges for churches in every age. Therefore, our discussion on Revelation will involve once again historical background from the first century.

## THE MEANING OF THE PASSAGE

The meaning of Revelation 3:16, 20 must depend on how we understand the letters. At the most basic level, the letter in question was written to a local church. At the broader level, the letter was also written to anyone who had ears (3:22). In other words, each letter also addressed every individual who was guilty of the crime charged by the letter. Thus, the seven letters have a representative function that goes beyond the seven churches to all churches in Asia Minor. In order to understand this passage, we must appreciate the function of such a passage. People commonly hold to this half-truth: the letters to the seven churches were written as a separate section of Revelation. Although it appears to be separate section, the seven letters indicate some of the challenges facing the churches that would be addressed by the rest of the book. Thus, the seven letters were ethical foundations of the book. Apocalyptic literature often has this veiled symbolic function. I believe that these letters are no exceptions. In order to understand the letter in question, we must understand the images contained within it by understanding what the audience saw and knew.

Laodicea is named after Laodice the wife of Antiochus II. Located in the southeast of ancient Philadelphia, this was the wealthiest city in the Phrygian area. Laodicea was known for its banks, clothing, and carpet. The city was so rich that they rebuilt the city after the AD 60 earthquakes without Rome's help. It also had a medical school where the Phrygian eye salve was made with special powder to heal eye ailment. Equally important is the geographical feature of the water supply to and around the city. The water supply of Laodicea came from the Hieropolis in the Lycus Valley where there are hot springs used for medical purposes. At the end of the stream was Colossae where the water was completely cleared of minerals and good for drinking. This geographical fact will illuminate the text greatly.

*Revelation 3:16, 20—Lukewarm? An Invitation to Unbelievers?*

John quickly jumped into speaking about the knowledge of Christ, in 3:15, explaining that Jesus knew about their "deeds" that revealed two spiritual conditions. First, Jesus knew that they were neither hot nor cold. The common interpretation that talks about "lukewarm" as a spiritual temperature is in fact wrong, based on the geographical fact above. Rather, the background is that Jesus would prefer that they were hot so that they could provide healing like the hot springs or cold so that they could give refreshment like the cold springs. Since they were neither, the church did not serve any function. Second, Jesus knew that they were lukewarm. In Laodicea, the church was like its water, lukewarm, which made it useless for healing or for sustaining life through drinks. Jesus was not talking about their spiritual temperature, but was talking about their uselessness. She had become a church with no purpose and no spiritual function. Jesus then accused them immediately. Jesus talked about the causes of their uselessness in 3:17: their mistaken notion that material wealth equated spiritual wealth. It was a self-satisfied church. Among the seven churches, this was the worst church, receiving no compliment from Christ.

Jesus provided two remedies in 3:18–19 for this desperately sick church. The way Jesus framed his remedies was completely tied to the city's material success. First, Jesus commanded them to "buy from me" in 3:18a. True wealth comes from Christ, and not from money. Jesus told them to buy white garments in 3:18b, in contrast to the black wool produced in the city. Jesus also told them to buy eye salve in 3:18b in order to see clearly and not like the earthly Phrygian powder. The earthly cures were no match for heavenly healing. The church could begin healing of its sickness by repenting.

The promise of Christ in 3:20–22 has two parts. Before the promise can be realized, certain conditions have to be right. This is where the contentious 3:20 is located. Even though some evangelistic tracts use 3:20 as a call to salvation, Christ was clearly talking to the church! In 3:20a, the door to the church was shut. In ancient cities, doors were used to keep enemies out. In any house, doors were also means of security to keep out thieves. Whether we view the church as the city of God or as a household, by using this imagery, Christ showed that he never became the church's enemy, but the church often made him the enemy. How was Christ outside the door of the church? Self-satisfied churches kept Christ out because they felt no need. So the door must be open first for any openness to Christ's solution. Once the door was open, a special meal could occur, but the church must overcome her self-satisfaction and arrogance. This fellowship was highly individual because Jesus uses the language of "to him . . . I . . ." Individual members still had a chance. The church however seems to have reached paralysis.

## APPLICATION

This is a great passage to apply simply because it shows that it is possible for Christians to shut out Jesus from their church gathering. As a result, churches reach a state of uselessness. The passage not only warns the Laodicean church, but also all churches. It demonstrates the insidious situation facing a wealthy church.

It is a well-known fact that in many parts of the world, the Christian church is primarily an upper middle-class entity. Certainly, on average, the US church is upper middle class. Based on the background of this church, churches that are financially well off are especially vulnerable. God is not against strong finances. Rather, he is against seeing financial wealth as equivalent to spiritual blessing. Many churches that preach this kind of success through numbers and finance are then forced to use many means to raise more money to maintain that successful image. This too is the road to the useless situation of Laodicea.

This is a prevalent and subtle prosperity gospel Christians preach. When they get rich, they say that they got it from God. We see this in testimony all the time, giving a kind of false impression that God blesses through riches. Whether we like it or not, riches can be only one way and by far not the best measurement of God's blessing. The most blessed church among the seven churches of Revelation may be Philadelphia, a church with little resources to speak of. John, in general, wrote the letter to the whole church, but he also talked of individuals by using "if anyone (singular) hears . . ." In light of this passage, I think Christians need to readjust their thinking and their witness, both in terms of entire churches and individuals.

## MISTAKES TO AVOID

The first mistake to avoid is the use of our own experience as the main tool to interpret a biblical analogy (lukewarm). This mistake can lead to a whole false theological system. In such a case, the system does not work well at all because it creates more problems. For instance, we may have to ask why Jesus preferred someone to be "cold," if we interpret the temperature as spiritual zeal for the gospel. There is no answer to that question because it is the wrong question to ask.

The second mistake to avoid is treating apocalyptic literature without the necessary background of the audience. When we use our own experience to interpret Scripture, there is a real danger of neglecting the audience's knowledge. Apocalyptic literature, like any other biblical writing, has the interest of the audience in mind. If the audience did not understand the images and messages associated with them, how would we be able to understand? The chapters below on Revelation 7 and 14 will illustrate this point well.

## DISCUSSION QUESTIONS

- What is wrong with the popular meanings?
- How does lukewarm apply to the church?
- What does the passage say about wealth and church?
- How does the meaning of the passage illuminate the Christian life?

# 27

# Revelation 7:1–17; 14:1–5—
# Israel and the Rapture Church?

"Do not harm the land or the sea or the trees until we put a seal on the foreheads of the servants of our God." Then I heard the number of those who were sealed: 144,000 from all the tribes of Israel....

Then I looked, and there before me was the Lamb, standing on Mount Zion, and with him 144,000 who had his name and his Father's name written on their foreheads....

## THE POPULAR MEANING

THERE ARE MANY POPULAR understandings of this passage. One very popular interpretation is to see the 144,000 to be national Israel while the great multitudes to be the church that had been take up in the rapture. Such an understanding is based on the plain sense of the text and has much to commend it. At the same time, the presupposition of a rapture, only taught in Paul's letters (e.g., 1 Thessalonians 4:17), is behind such an interpretation. This presupposition deserves scrutiny. We need to ask a question. Did John's audience in Revelation know Paul's teaching? Did they have to know Paul's teaching in order to understand Revelation 7 and 14, or is it possible to interpret John's work based on the ground rules set by the book of Revelation without harmonizing John with Paul? We shall answer the question below.

*Revelation 7:1-17; 14:1-5—Israel and the Rapture Church?*

## WHERE DOES THE PASSAGE BEGIN?

Revelation is an ongoing narrative about John's vision. This is definitely the plain reading of the text. Whether or not we associate it with a few editing processes, the text as it stands shows a man experiencing a vision. Revelation 7 and 14 belong to the vision section that follows the letters to the seven churches. Revelation 7 belongs to the section on the seals in 6:1—8:5. Revelation 14 belongs to the section of the trumpets in 8:6—14:20. Thereafter is the section on the bowls of wrath in 15:1—19:10. Each section includes an intermission. For example, Revelation 7 is the intermission of the seal vision, while Revelation 14 belongs to the long intermission that describes the war between Christ's army and the anti-Christ in chapters 11–14. It is interesting that both texts in question belong to the intermissions of their respective sections. Thus, we should look at Revelation 7 as the high point of transition to the section of the trumpets in 8:6. Since it is a narrative, we must set Revelation 7 within its own very large section (6:1—8:4). The same goes for Revelation 14 (8:6—14:20).

## THE MEANING OF THE PASSAGE

This is a passage that seriously challenges our understanding of the numbering system of John in Revelation. In accordance to our overall principle of sticking to the author's interpretive tendencies, we need to understand John's numbering system. It is worth spending some time exploring the unique (but consistent) numbering system of Revelation. Two methodological principles govern the meaning of this passage. First, we must deal with the numbering system because it dominates the passage. Second, we must deal with the ethnic label of Israel because that too dominates the passage.

There is certain logic in the numbering system of Revelation consistent throughout. Revelation shows a clear pattern as to how numbering should be interpreted. The book has consistent rules. Here are some examples that are closely related to this passage. The number seven, which occurs frequently, denotes perfection. The number twelve and its multiples denote God's people. The number six is a malevolent portrait of humanity. The number ten denotes multitudes. The more zeros are added at the end of any number (e.g., 144,000), the greater the multitude. The number four denotes the four directions from which events come. Thus, whatever the ultimate conclusion we draw about numbers, we must never overlook their consistent symbolic significance. We must respect the numbering system and not break rules at our own whim. We shall make the above numberings system the working hypothesis of this work.

After looking at the numbering, we also need to look at how names function in Revelation because John used "Israel" to describe these people on earth. It is hard to understand whether John means for Israel here to be symbolic. We must compare this name with the way John used other names in order for us to find a solution. John's strategy in naming something lends itself to symbolism. In every case of a named character, the name itself is symbolic. "Babylon" seems to be symbolic of Rome. Surely, "Jerusalem" at the last two chapters of Revelation is symbolic because it ends up not being a city but a group of people (e.g., the Lamb, the apostles, the twelve tribes, etc.). If we keep in mind the exile text from which John seems to have drawn to describe this vision, we must not miss the obvious; Israel is set in contrast to pagan Babylon. The microscopic analysis without a macroscopic perspective is incomplete at best and warped at worst. We may now look at the passage in some of its details.

We must first note that John did not get the number 144,000 by counting. He is told the number (7:4). The exactness of the number of each tribe also calls into question whether these are literally Jews because John had no way to identify these people visually until he heard their number and identity being called out in 7:4–8. He later recycles the 144,000 in Revelation 14 in contrast with the number of the beast. Furthermore, John had the exact number of members in each tribe as multiples of twelve, which we have already discussed above indicates the symbolism of God's people.

The lack of clarity in Revelation 7 seems to be cleared up by Revelation 14. For now, we must see that further evidence suggests that the specificity of the names also contributes to understanding the identity of the 144,000. The curious fact is the prominent place Judah had in the vision by heading the list, fitting perfectly the "lion of Judah" messianic motif of 5:5. This order of having Judah at the head is merely building on what is already revealed in the vision of 5:5. Dan and Ephraim were also curiously omitted, both replaced by Joseph. The best guess is that John's vision needs the number twelve. Some say that the replacement has to do with idolatry. After all, idolatry was a serious problem among his Asia Minor churches (e.g., Revelation 2:14, 20, etc.). Thus, 144,000 is the symbol of all those who refused to yield to idolatry due to their identity with God. John's use of thousands

## Revelation 7:1-17; 14:1-5—Israel and the Rapture Church?

is normally an expression of vastness. With it being linked to the square of twelve, John uses the number creatively to show the vastness of all who belong to God. God knows every one of them because he alone knows their number. The contrast between the sections Revelation 7:1-8 and 7:9-17 is not about ethnicity, but location. 7:1-8 represents the elect on earth while 7:9-12 represents those already in God's heavenly court.

On the balance of evidence, we must see 144,000 as a symbol of the church militant on earth rather than merely Jews on earth. The numbering serves a different purpose to show an exact number of elect only God knew. God knows every elect individual. Set within 6:1—8:5, this number shows a degree of protection for the elect on earth, not so much from any persecution, but from the wrath of the Lamb in 6:17. Based on our line of reasoning, the 144,000 and the unnumbered multitudes in heaven were the same kind of people: the people of God. The only difference, as I pointed out just now, was location. Why then would there be no numbering in the heavens? This should be the next question asked. The answer is quite simple. There is no need for numbering in heaven because there is no war. The reason why John needed numbering was to create a theme. The reason for John's system would become clearer in Revelation 14. Numbering denotes preparation for war where soldiers were numbered. The numbering of the tribes to enter Canaan was for military purposes in the Old Testament.

It is now time to look at Revelation 14:1-5. The story is part of the ongoing war between Christ's army and Satan's. Here, the function of the elect is to contrast against those who have the mark of the beast. Besides numbering them 144,000, the sealing of God's people here functions as the contrast to 13:16-18 where the foreheads of idolaters have "666" on them. The numbering of 666 will surely prove that numbering is symbolic. John did not assume that everyone could figure out the symbolic numbering but only those who had "insights" (13:18). What insight was he talking about? In John's day, there was a numbering system among the Hebrews that assigned numbers to the letters of their alphabet. For example, if we were to use the English alphabet for illustration, 1 would represent A, 2 would be B, and 3 would be C. When we hit J, then we move to 10, with K being 20 and so on. If "Nero Caesar" was transliterated into Hebrew, then his the numbers associated with the letters in his name add up to 666. There is some kind of link between the name and number of the beast based on 13:17. Here it also elaborates the fact that "it is the man's number." The emphasis then is more than mere calculation of the number. Rather, it's dealing with discernment of evil coming out of human government, exemplified in the first persecutor of Christians in the Empire, Nero Caesar. The persecution carried on sporadically into Domitian's reign.

What did the seal mean in ancient times? This is an important question to ask because of what was mentioned in 7:3 in contrast to the seal here in 13:18. In ancient times, the function of a seal was to authenticate. John's readers could see tattooed slaves walking around their streets. Maybe there were also slaves among John's audience who understood this image perfectly. It may be a metaphor for saying that God has set his hand of approval on these who will not be harmed. John then turns his attention to the elect in 14:1–5. Who then were the 144,000? They were *true* Israel in contrast to the *false* Jews of 2:9 and 3:9. The number of the remnant was not terribly small either based on the many multiples of ten in the number 144,000.

There is also something quite strange about the vision here in chapter 14 because of the discussion of sexuality. Why does the vision discuss the purity of 144,000 in terms of sexuality? If we were to take the image literally, it could be a group full of men without women. I do not believe John was speaking literally regarding sexuality. If we keep in mind the sexual imageries of Revelation, the answer is quite easy. 14:4a is a picture of religious purity as opposed to the whore, Babylon (14:8). One well-known symbol of the empire is the goddess Roma (where the name Rome came from). This symbolic woman was transformed by John into the sinister city called Babylon. Rome is not the goddess Roma but the "great whore" (Revelation 17)! The function of sexual image has been consistently religious and not sexual throughout Revelation (e.g., 2:14, 20; cf. 9:20–21; 21:8; 22:15). John linked sexual purity to an ideological holy war in Revelation between those who followed Jesus and those who followed Satan.

What then is this picture doing in light of 8:6—14:20? It is showing the strength and characteristics of God's army. This army was well prepared for war, not of its own strength but because of its election by the almighty God (7:3). Their greatest blessing was not the avoidance of earthly pain, but the embrace of heavenly reward. In light of the suffering church in Revelation, this vision was not predicting that there would be some future group of 144,000 Jews. In fact, a prediction of the future would do the first-century audience not much good. The vision came from what the audience knew at their time. It does not serve modern obsessions with "end times" or "left behind" scenarios. Rather, it brings together images of the Bible and first-century society to inform and encourage the first-century audience. In the midst of suffering, triumph would be the ultimate result.

## APPLICATION

Both texts discussed here are very much encouraging for the suffering church. Once we get through the jungle of interpretation, the passages are really quite simple and easily applicable. They speak of the Christian identity.

As the people of God, they are aliens in this world. Like the twelve tribes of Israel, they are in a new exodus. Like the exiles, they are waiting for liberation. It is a mistake for them to compromise because in warfare against Satan's system, there is no compromise. As a people of God, the church has a responsibility to exist as an army representing God in this world. In the complicated world we live in, it is an easy temptation to give in to the world's system. To John, it is not enough just to profess Jesus Christ. It is equally important for Christians and the church to live out the identity that is uniquely theirs.

## MISTAKES TO AVOID

The first mistake to avoid is breaking the author's numbering system. Meanings of numbers cannot be arbitrarily assigned based on the whims of the interpreter. The text itself should have a consistent system of signs and meanings. The interpreter's job is to read and reread the text so that he can finally figure out that system.

Another mistake to avoid is very subtle. The literal meaning of each symbol is important because it is from the literal ideas within the symbol that derive its meaning. The dichotomy between literal and symbolic is perhaps too strong a distinction. Rather, the literal is always the starting point but is not always the ending point.

The third mistake to avoid is the failure to look at function of names in apocalyptic literature. Names are not merely names. They are meant to do something within the context. It is not enough just to know that a name is there. Rather, it is more important to note why it is there and how the author uses it. Interpretation without appreciation for the rhetoric of the text will end up producing strange meanings.

## DISCUSSION QUESTIONS

- What is wrong with understanding the numbers and names literally?
- What is the purpose of names?
- What is the purpose of numbers?
- How do these passages address the modern Christian?

# 28

# Revelation 22:18–19—Subtracting from the Canon?

I warn everyone who hears the words of the prophecy of this scroll: If anyone adds anything to them, God will add to that person the plagues described in this scroll. And if anyone takes words away from this scroll of prophecy, God will take away from that person any share in the tree of life and in the Holy City, which are described in this scroll.

## THE POPULAR MEANING

REVELATION 22:19 IS OUR last, but not least, abused text in our sample of apocalyptic texts. The popular interpretation is to treat the verse as referring to the entire Bible. It goes something like this. The Bible is inerrant. Therefore, anyone who eliminates or adds to it will suffer divine punishment. Let us now lay aside whether this interpretation fits certain church dogma. Let us just face the very meaning of the text. Did the original readers understand this text according to the popular interpretation or are there other ways to read this text?

## WHERE DOES THE PASSAGE BEGIN?

The passage belongs to the last part of Revelation, starting from 22:6. The reason we can determine this is because of some of its unique vocabulary, occurring in the beginning of the book and nowhere else (cf. 22:13; 1:8, 17).

Furthermore, some translations put 22:7 as the beginning of the last section. This is less than ideal because 22:7 is still part of the angel's conversation in 22:6. It is therefore good to see 22:18–19 as part of the epilogue of the book.

## THE MEANING OF THE PASSAGE

At this stage, the reading of the text should be quite straightforward. If the rest of the vocabulary was drawn from the reader's world, this text surely would make sense to the readers. We have to understand that the formation of the New Testament canon was a complex, drawn out, and careful process. It is, therefore, not ideal to read the entire canon of the Bible or even the New Testament into 22:18–19. I am not at all suggesting that we can add or subtract from the canon, but such was not the point of John because the New Testament canon was not even established yet. What then is John's point?

In order to appreciate John's point fully, we must return to our previous thought about this as being a reflection of the prologue's vocabulary. After editing the entire text of Revelation, maybe several times, John probably added the beginning and the end in matching pair because the head and tail of this book contain unique vocabulary. By doing so, he summarized the true message of the book. He wanted the audience not to miss certain truths even though, perhaps, some sections were difficult to understand.

In looking at this ending, there is a sense of finality both in blessing and in curses. For instance, 22:10–12 shows the abandonment of the cursed. The book remains open according to the message, as opposed to a closed book like Daniel, because the time is near. The opened book was there for repeated reading for John's audience because the time was near.

Here is some common ground between the beginning and the end of the book. The main points of this vision are found in 22:12–20a. First, it shows who Jesus is, in 22:12–13. The theme here was already found in 1:8, 17, so this may be a reminder of the prologue. It is interesting that Jesus is described as "the beginning and the end" at the beginning and the end of the book. Jesus had spoken all that he needed to say about the end of the first-century situation. This is what the attributes of Jesus mean in the book's context.

Second, the vision shows what Jesus did in 22:14–15. 22:14 shows blessedness/happiness for those who keep their identity clean, since clothing shows identity. They receive "authority" which is originally privileged to

God (16:19). Jesus paid them back by letting them reign with God (22:12–14). The non-believers received curses. We have to remember that these sayings are written with the Roman Empire in mind, where its Asia Minor citizens alienated and persecuted Christians. Jesus was pronouncing judgment based on this first-century background. Alienation and acceptance were the dominant themes. The reversal of roles now happened at the end in favor of the Christians and in disfavor against their persecutors. During the Christians' alienation from the world, they found acceptance in Christ.

Third, the vision shows Jesus' provision in 22:16–20a. The basis of any provision is the kingly character of Jesus. 22:16 shows his continued kingship. Jesus' provision of water contrasts well against the water of the Roman aqueducts. Within these images of the empire, Jesus showed the superiority of his kingdom against worldly resources. It is at this juncture that we look at the text in question. The verses in 22:18–19 warn of the authenticity and importance of this message. Why indeed did John want to talk about this aspect? I would say that the rampant heresies within his time had certainly put a damper on the early Christian church. This problem continued well after John's death. Jesus demanded care in dealing with the teaching contained in this writing. Although this is where the canon closes, the intent of the warning has nothing to do with the canon for the reasons already discussed. It is also curious that Jesus directed this towards the audience, although he said "anyone" because after all, the first recipients were Christians. In other words, the church might have contained those who held the truth loosely. John ended the narrative with an invitation for Jesus to come. The coming of Jesus first would condemn those who were active enemies of the church. He would further demolish heretical ideas. Then, he would provide comfort to his followers who would enter the eternal rest.

## APPLICATION

There are many things we can learn from this passage. It is a wonderful passage to show that the truth is always in danger even within the church. Jesus held the church responsible for being careful in handling the truth of Revelation. In the same way, there is no way we can stand by and say, "That is not my business." Furthermore, the church should take truth so seriously that she should not let up in her search for truth, even if she might not like what she finds.

Based on the background, Jesus' provision is so much better than what the world can offer. This is an important idea to note. Quite often, Christians live as if the world's provision is all that they ever need. This chapter counters against such a mentality. Jesus' future provision ought to be the present hope for Christians. Those who lust after the provision of the world have lost the vision of that hope. As a result, they have shipwrecked their faith.

## MISTAKES TO AVOID

The first mistake to avoid is the problem of not reading the text in context. Apocalyptic literature is complex enough without adding further problems by reading without context. The narration of the entire book should give some limit as to what are possible meanings and what are not.

The second mistake to avoid is the lack of understanding of background and how it should enlighten the text. Among all biblical literature, background is perhaps most important in reading apocalyptic because without it, it is impossible to understand the text at all. Whatever the audience could not grasp, the modern interpreter surely cannot. Thus, any interpretation ought to flow out of the world of the original audience and not from our own fantasy.

## DISCUSSION QUESTIONS

- What is the problem with seeing the ending of Revelation as the closing of the canon?
- What is the emphasis by John at the ending?
- How does the background of Revelation explain better the meaning of the epilogue?
- How does the message address today's church?

# Conclusion

WITH SUCH AN ABUNDANT pool of samples, we can now summarize the pitfalls to avoid when reading the New Testament.

## MISTAKES IN SERMON INTERPRETATION

In dealing with Jesus' sermons, many treat them like Paul's letters. While they do have a propositional flavor about them, they do not, in the main, read well as letters. The main difference is that each sermon has its own narrative context from which its truth was taught. What I mean is that surrounding the sermon, there is a storyline that gave birth to the sermon. We can often find the ancient occasion that caused Jesus (and sometimes his followers) to preach a sermon. Each narrative context demands the interpreter's care. So, the first and primary mistake in dealing with New Testament sermons is the lack of care towards the narrative context, including where the narrative begins and ends. This marks the first and most fatal mistake in understanding sermons.

The second mistake made is the lack of care taken to define terms and concepts based on the sermon itself. As we have stated, the ideas within the sermon are meant to enhance and carry the sermon. Thus, before we determine the meaning of the passage based on content, we must think about how the passage is being used in relation to the rest of the sermon, just like the prayer passage in Matthew 7:7–12 is not about prayer but about divine grace and justice.

The third mistake made is a lack of understanding of the book context. Sometimes, mistakes can be quite critical when certain New Testament books have clear narrative and literary structures that provide clear interpretive guidelines (e.g., Matthew, John). Ignoring this is a fatal mistake because without this context, there is no determining guideline to judge whether the interpreter is close or not. All interpreters are limited in their

*Conclusion*

understanding when it comes to meaning simply because they are human, but sound guidelines can at least show what is *not* the meaning.

## MISTAKES IN NARRATIVE INTERPRETATION

In looking at narratives, many take stories only as historical facts without appreciating what the author was doing creatively with the story. Several important factors need to be considered when reading narratives.

What qualifies a genre as narrative? First, there must be a narrator who narrates the account. Second, the narrator provides the flow of the story. Third, in order for a text to be a narrative, it has to have characters within who play their parts.

The first mistake in looking at narrative is failing to recognize the development of the plot. This means that the interpreter needs to understand where the narrative begins. In a sense, the entire book (e.g., John) is one long narrative that does not break. This is true. Yet, within the grand narrative are many smaller narratives. These narratives fit together like a puzzle to create the grand narrative. Thus, the very first step in analyzing the narrative is to find out how each small narrative begins and ends. This is a task that has been repeatedly demonstrated throughout this book. My observation is that many preachers still refuse to use this step to their advantage. Only after analyzing the singular narrative event can the interpreter link up with the grand narrative the author has created.

Another mistake in looking at narrative is ignoring the narrator's comments. Some prefer to call it the author's comments. Whatever we wish to call it, the bottom line is quite often the narrator's comments give an indicator as to why the story was recorded in the first place. I often use one example from John 2:6, where the Jewish jars of ceremonial washing provide the full Jewish color for the narrative, reflecting the concern over ceremonial washing that has been transformed by Jesus Christ. Most people take the comment as a fact, but if the event links well with the temple story that follows, then the meaning is not merely factual. The comment is the author's hint as to what he thought about the Jewish ceremonialism.

One final common mistake is the lack of effort in distinguishing reliable characters. I say this because there are some characters within certain narratives that are clearly reliable. Their comments count for more than other unreliable characters. If we are to look at the narrator as a character, he is a reliable character. His comments count for a lot, based on the discussion in the previous paragraph. Characters such as Jesus or sometimes the apostles (in most cases in Acts) are also reliable characters. Their words also count for quite a lot. When reading narrative, we must not treat all characters equally, as flat characters. Some have more credibility than others. Interpretation should come from their perspectives and not the perspectives of the minor characters.

## MISTAKES IN LETTER INTERPRETATION

The first mistake made in dealing with letters is treating each part of the letter as if it were unrelated to other parts of the letter. Sections of the letter are not static entities only made for modern inductive Bible studies on doctrinal issues. These are *real* letters addressing real problems. Explanation of any section must also explain surrounding sections. Even if a sentence seems independent, no sentence is truly independent from context. If the interpreter does not respect context, the interpretation is incomplete at best, and wrong at worst.

The second mistake in studying letters is treating them as bare propositions without consideration of the situational and historical backgrounds. Letters like Romans and Ephesians seem highly propositional and doctrinal. But they are not theological treatises. However, even though they are not theological treatises, these biblical authors still wrote in a coherent and logical manner. They address real church problems. Just because there was no conflict in a church, does not mean that the letter writer did not have a background in mind.

The third mistake in studying letters is a lack of awareness of the authorial purpose. This is not hard to correct. Most letters in the ancient times speak of the author's purpose at the beginning of the letter. Certainly, this is the case with just about every Pauline letter. Quite frequently, the purpose can also be supplemented by the ending of the letter. It is in these two parts that the author clearly shows his relationship with the audience. We can guess from there what the purpose is. Yet, these are two of the most neglected parts of reading a letter. The good news is, it is easy to correct.

The fourth mistake in studying letters is forgetting their community function. Paul's usage of plural pronouns to address readers should alert the modern interpreter. Many modern interpreters turn Paul's letters into some kind of moralistic application for individuals. This negates the corporate impact the gospel must have had in the eyes of all New Testament writers.

*Conclusion*

The reception of a letter was a public event, when a literate person read the material out loud to the congregation. Letters were not meant for one person (except for 1 and 2 Timothy, perhaps). The impact should be public and corporate.

## MISTAKES IN APOCALYPTIC INTERPRETATION

Strictly speaking, the only apocalyptic literature in the Bible is Revelation. There are many mistakes made regarding Revelation that deserve serious contemplation. First, some suppose that many separate the letters form the entire book. This is a grave mistake. In 1:4, John stated that the entire book is a singular letter written to the seven churches. The individual letters in chapters 2 and 3 merely point out specific struggles of each church that can also infect the other churches. In other words, within the letters of the seven churches, John stated the problems that will be addressed by the rest of the book. This is not something we should take lightly. Most pastors who preach Revelation only touch on the first three chapters while missing the solutions in the rest of the book.

Second, it is important to take seriously the narrative aspect of the book. The entire book is a narration of John's vision. It reads like a very strange story, but still, it is a story. With a story, there is a plot, starting with the origin of the story (e.g., the seven letters stating the problems), progressing through various dramas (e.g., Satan versus Christ, etc.), and concluding with some results (e.g., New Jerusalem). When people pick and choose bits of the narrative and make theology out of them, they will no doubt come up with something quite strange and alien from John's true vision. If we track the book as one gigantic story, we can then make greater meaning of its parts. In other words, when we study one part or another, we have to ask how this part is related to all the other parts of the narrative.

Third, like any apocalyptic literature, the background behind the text is very important because there are a whole lot of hidden symbols in apocalyptic literature that the original audience could figure out but that the casual modern interpreter no longer can. Those who insist on a meaning without necessary background data will make big mistakes. The final and most basic issue is still the audience's knowledge. What did the audience know and when did the audience know it?

## CONCLUSION: LOOKING FORWARD

After one particular course on the New Testament as a visiting professor in a seminary, a fellow minister came up to me afterwards and told me that my course had completely waken him up from his exegetical slumber. I'm glad to be of service. I certainly do not have all the answers (or even most of the answers) about the New Testament, but I hope the issues and questions I bring out will cause the interpreter to take God's word more seriously.

After another seminar on biblical interpretation, a former student told me (much to my disappointment) that it's "too hard" to exegete and preach properly. Of course it is too hard when one has been reading out of context for years. It is like trying to heal the heroin addict of his addiction. Such addicts will suffer withdrawal. Others may even revert to their old habits. A person who recovers will have to work twice as hard to get rid of the original instinct. It takes more to get rid of bad habits than to cultivate good ones.

When writing and teaching about the topic at hand, I'm reminded of an analogy I heard from a famous professor. After hearing about all the great stuff the professor had taught, many of his students remarked that the material was indeed great, but when push came to shove, they would probably fall back on their original theological instincts. This is exactly what I'm afraid of. This book will meet its biggest failure if my readers resort to default mode when encountering passages of the Bible. It would be as if an unwashed and unkempt man looked into the mirror, realized that he looked terrible, and then moved on without ever grooming and washing himself.

Recently, in a public lecture on exegetical fallacy, a young lady despaired, "Dr. Tsang, I experience true fear now that I know about my mistakes. I now hesitate to lead any more Bible study." Her sentiment is understandable and normal. Fear and reverence are good when the interpreter approaches Scripture. However, I encouraged her to keep up her effort without paralyzing fear. It is like learning to break a bad habit. It will take time, but the worst thing is to give up before the new process becomes second nature.

My greatest hope for this book is that my readers will experience a change in exegetical mentality. This is especially applicable for those who preach in the pulpit or lead Bible studies, but is also applicable to the general reader of the Bible who seeks to spend time daily reading the "word of God." If this book contributes to helping them not take any Bible passage

## Conclusion

for granted, I am already satisfied. There is a whole lot of interpretation from our church background that should be cherished, but there is also a whole lot that deserves renewed evaluation. My hope is that every reader of this book will not merely fall back on to his original instinct, but will take the path less traveled of looking at Scriptural context closely. If people will just get one lesson from this book, it should be the importance of context. If every reader of this book will learn to work harder on the context of the text, my work is not in vain. I close this book with an encouragement from Quintilian's conclusion to his great work, *The Education of an Orator* (12.11.31), "If the knowledge of these principles proves to be of small practical utility to the student, it should at least produce what I value more, the will to do well." May we all do better!

www.ingramcontent.com/pod-product-compliance
Lightning Source LLC
Chambersburg PA
CBHW071515150426
43191CB00009B/1534